D1535710

ECONOMICOLOGY II

by Peter M. Wege

EDITOR
Susan Lovell, The Wege Foundation

BOOK & COVER DESIGN
Sherri Days

PROOFREADER
Deborah Johnson Wood

SPECIAL THANKS TO
Without an editor, a book is almost without a
cover, so I would like to thank my editor Susan
Lovell for her guidance over the past few years
in keeping me moving ahead. Thank you Susan,
it would have been tough without your guidance.
Terri McCarthy, Ellen Satterlee, & Brandie Perry of
The Wege Foundation; Mark Van Putten, President
of ConservationStrategy LLC & Past President of
National Wildlife Federation; Mike Bardwell and
Jason Bardwell of D&D Printing Company; Chuck
Oleniczak of Central Michigan Paper.

MOHAWK windpower

Published by The Wege Foundation,
a Michigan nonprofit corporation
P.O. Box 6388
Grand Rapids, Michigan 49516

This book is printed on Mohawk Options, 100%
PC which is manufactured entirely with Green-e
certified wind-generated electricity.

Mohawk Options, 100% PC contains 100%
postconsumer waster fiber.

Library of Congress Control Number: 2009944155

ISBN-13: 978-0-615-34544-4

Mohawk Options, 100% PC is certified by
Green Seal, a non-profit organization devoted
to environmental standard setting, product
cerfitication, and environmental education.

Do all the good you can
for as many people as you
can for as long as you can.

Peter M. Wege

I would like to dedicate this book to all current and future students enrolled in colleges, universities, and schools of higher learning.

I also dedicate this book to their teachers and professors who should be recognized and honored by all of us. They are my heroes for taking on brave causes to help solve world problems.

Peter M. Wege

The Man Behind
ECONOMICOLOGY II

by Susan Lovell

Peter M. Wege, author of this second book on economicology, is many things to many people. A thinker. A visionary. An optimist. A prophet. An environmentalist. A philanthropist. A giver. An author. A poet. And a joke teller.

He was born February 19, 1920, in Grand Rapids, Michigan, where he has lived his life. In 1941, he set a freshman record in the javelin throw at the University of Michigan before joining the Army Air Force after Pearl Harbor. Lt. Wege flew planes for four years, returning home in 1946 to join the family business, Metal Office Furniture then – Steelcase, Inc. today.

This veteran pilot, this person of deep spirituality, has always been ahead of his time in speaking out and writing about threats to the environment. For over forty years he has been asking his fellow Americans the rhetorical question, "Is the planet worth saving?" In 1968, he created The Wege Foundation with the first mission to clean up his hometown's water, air, and soil.

Peter Wege helped bring environmental awareness into mainstream thinking by defining it as a matter of economics as well. "Economicology," the title of this book, is a word he coined that blends the word "economy" with the word "ecology." A business man himself, Wege recognized the need to incorporate economics into the environmental movement. His mantra has been that a profitable economy requires a healthy ecology.

He has promoted this concept of economicology through his support for education, both K-12 and at the college level. He wrote the book you are reading for the same reason. As he puts it, the purpose of this book is, "To educate! Educate! Educate!" In these pages, he draws on just a few of the many environmental thinkers he has studied. His hope is that after you finish *ECONOMICOLOGY II,* you will go look up the writers he has quoted and read their entire books for yourselves.

One inside story of how effective Peter Wege's leadership has been is not in this book. But it started when Peter Wege first insisted that any capital gift from The Wege Foundation must seek United States Green Building Council certification. As a result, Grand Rapids is now the top city in the United States for the amount of LEED-certified building square-feet per person.

Another inside story behind his largest single gift reveals his character. Peter Wege gave Grand Rapids the first LEED-certified art museum in the world. The generosity of his gift moved the Grand Rapids Art Museum board to ask that the museum be renamed the Wege Art Museum. His reply, "Absolutely not!" He thanked the GRAM board for the offer, then said, "This art museum does not belong to the Wege family. It belongs to the people of Grand Rapids. That's how the name will stay."

His family has always been important to Peter. In 1912, his father Peter Martin Wege founded today's Steelcase, the largest office-furniture manufacturer in the world. And Peter never stops giving his father and mother Sophia Louise full credit for teaching him the moral principle of generosity and for providing the material resources that have allowed him do so much good.

Peter Wege's favorite saying summarizes his life's work: "Do all the good you can for all the people you can for as long as you can."

Contents

Prologue

I have been thinking about all the books I've read since college. For me, the authors' literary merits have never been as important as the wisdom they share is. Honest evaluation of the best authors I have read, and included in this book *ECONOMICOLOGY II*, has led me to a valuable conclusion: common sense is the basic approach all these authors take. And common sense is the best course of action for the rest of us to follow.

Having lived a full life, and having gone through World War II as an Air Force pilot experiencing several close calls, I have tried to understand life's purpose. I have lived through confusing times, good times, and bad times. And what have I figured out?

I don't know why we are on Earth, but what I believe to be our highest value is having faith in a Supreme Being. We stretch our thinking on the ultimate purpose of life. But with our finite brains, we can only try to imagine the infinite mind of this Divine Being whom I call God.

That faith leads me to the next purpose of our lives on Earth. Bringing up our families and caring for our relatives and friends is a major reason we are here in the first place. We are also here to do what I have said for my entire adult life: **to do all the good we can for as many people as we can for as long as we can.**

Writing this book is part of what I am doing to

accomplish that mission. Saving the planet requires us to unite all the universities in the world from every major country. But it is important that the scholarly thinking that comes out of these universities is free from any government control.

We are at a time when educated and intelligent people worldwide need to begin promoting and teaching positive thinking. All people yearn for peace and cooperative growth among nations of the world. Since 1949, the United Nations has tried to do this. But there have been too many countries working only for their own interests rather than for the betterment of the world as a whole.

It takes an educated populace a long time to come together for all the right reasons. But that time seems to be now. The question is whether or not we have the willpower to overcome the negative and hopeless attitudes and replace them with positive and hopeful thinking for true world peace.

Do we have the world intelligence to make that happen?

I hope this book helps you, the reader, answer that with a big: **YES WE DO!**

PETER'S PRINCIPLES OF ECONOMICOLOGY

Create a balance of livability between our ecology and the economy: economicology!

Create positive thinking!

Create understanding of why we are here!

Create friendship instead of animosity!

Create a union of educated nations in a force that can help everyone!

End war forever!

CHAPTER 1

Red Sky at Morning: America and the Crisis of the Global Environment

Americans used to have a devout, passionate belief in the future. Where did it go? A political leader asked me what was the most important thing any leader could do for the American people today, and I said, 'Give them back their future!'

John W. Gardner, Stanford Centennial Speech
September 29, 1991

Since the 1998 publication of my first book *ECONOMICOLOGY: The Eleventh Commandment,* I have come across several other important environmental thinkers who are carrying on the great mission of my hero John W. Gardner. This sequel to my first book will highlight some of the latest economicology thinking from these bright environmental leaders.

As I did in my 1998 ECONOMICOLOGY, I have used leading environmental authors who all work from research and statistics. These are academicians and scientists, not alarmists. They would not write what they have if it weren't true. They are some of the best environmental thinkers who are carrying on John W. Gardner's charge to 'give Americans back their future.'

The first is Dr. James Gustave 'Gus' Speth, Yale University Dean and Professor in Environmental Policy and Sustainable Development. My friend Gus is a national authority on economicology, which is the interaction of the economy and the environment.

Dr. Speth is a Yale graduate and Rhodes Scholar who chaired the White House Council on Environmental Quality under President Jimmy Carter.

One of Speth's most significant accomplishments was co-founding the Natural Resources Defense Council – perhaps this country's most influential organization in crafting the nation's environmental policies. Dr. Speth went on to found the World Resources Institute bringing together world leaders to use scientific evidence in addressing the issues that threaten the Earth's ecosystems.

Gus Speth signing books during the 10th Annual Wege Lecture Series at Aquinas College, photo courtesy of the Photography Room

Gus Speth is the author of *Red Sky At Morning: America and The Crisis of the Global Environment.* When I read this book in late 2005, I called Yale and invited Dr. Speth to be the keynote speaker for the 10th annual Wege Lecture Series at Aquinas College. In April 2006, Gus Speth came to my home city and spoke to an auditorium full of interested West Michigan residents. His talk to a cross-section of my fellow citizens was a good condensation of his book and an encouragement for them to read Red Sky for themselves.

Just as John Gardner did and I have tried to do, Gus Speth reaches out to the young people who hold the future of our planet in their hands. As Speth wrote in the beginning of *Red Sky At Morning:*

> My fondest hope is that this will be a book widely read by young people. Those of us who began our careers in the environmental issues of the late 1960s and early 1970s are approaching retirement. I eagerly accepted Yale's offer to be dean of its environment school to make contact with the new generation and to contribute back what I have learned, so that they might benefit from what we got right and not repeat our numerous mistakes.

I particularly like Speth's thinking because he does not focus on all our environmental problems. Instead, he writes in hopeful terms about possible solutions. For instance, Speth writes about what could be accomplished through an international treaty like the 1997 Kyoto Protocol protecting the climate. The Kyoto Protocol required industrial nations to reduce their greenhouse gas emissions to at least five percent below their levels in 1990. Speth calls it "the first international treaty with any teeth in it" that addresses climate change.

Unfortunately, former President George W. Bush rejected Kyoto – which applied only to industrialized countries. But, the negative outcry from the international community forced him to respond. The President's answer was to find out if global warming really was a threat by passing the treaty on to the National Academy of Sciences (NAS) for review. But if President Bush expected the NAS to conclude that global warming does not endanger the planet, he did not get the reply he was looking for. Indeed, the

NAS's findings contradicted those who argue that global warming is a hoax and, therefore, the Kyoto Protocol is not necessary. Instead, this high-powered Academy of scientists concluded just the opposite.

> NAS reported back to the White House that greenhouse gases are accumulating in earth's atmosphere as a result of human activities... human-induced warming and sea-level rise will continue into the next century...global warming could well have serious adverse societal and ecological impacts by the end of this century.

As I write this in late 2009, the Kyoto Treaty is about to expire and we have a new national leader in President Barack Obama who is a bona fide economicologist. Obama understands we cannot have a prosperous economy without a healthy ecology. The treaty to replace Kyoto will be written in Copenhagen, and the United States Congress is already working on laws to decrease the amount of CO_2 and other greenhouse gases we produce. As the world's greatest contributor to global-warming pollution, we can't go to Copenhagen telling India and China they have to lower their CO_2 emissions if we aren't going to do the same!

What Gus Speth wrote about the Kyoto protocol in *Red Sky At Morning* applies just as much to the new Copenhagen Treaty:

> The United States should join the Kyoto process both because America is the largest emitter of climate pollution and...the Kyoto Protocol is the best means we have for beginning to reduce climate-altering emissions...

Gus Speth's book goes on to summarize eight specific steps that could lead us away from environmental destruction and toward sustainability. His number one recommendation is a plea I've been making for years. We must control our population growth. Gus

Speth calls it "A Stable or Smaller World Population." His book lists a series of global organizations working on this goal – along with their web sites – including People and the Planet, The Population Council, and Population Action International.

The headline over the lead letter to the editor in the Grand Rapids Press on October 12, 2006, read: *Control overpopulation* and was signed, Peter Wege/ East Grand Rapids. Gus Speth and I are on the same page naming the number-one cause of our planet's environmental degradation. This is my letter published in the Press:

> Overpopulation is killing this planet, literally, and the leadership of the world is powerless to do anything about it. China is trying to do the best they can under the circumstances, because they understand the problem. But politically and religiously, they are powerless to create a government that can start to cure the problem.
>
> The U.S. government is trying to figure out how to deal with immigration. Closing our borders is the only viable solution until we work out the problem of how many should be allowed into our country and for all the right reasons. They have to want to become loyal American citizens.
>
> We finally have to figure how many people we can support based on our ability to provide a healthy and viable living experience.
>
> This has to be based on the availability of natural resources and the farms to supply an adequate food supply, and the kind of democratic government that provides the kind of life the majority of our voting citizens feel is necessary for this to happen.

I urge you to read *Red Sky At Morning*. But you need to read it all the way through, not piecemeal. Don't be surprised if the reading is difficult, because

Speth covers many environmental topics definitively and in detail.

At the same time, you will be pleasantly surprised at his background facts because he is so good at emphasizing the most important and informative material. Indeed, it's hard to read any page that is not explicit.

As I write about these extremely important authors, it's hard to translate the excitement of their provocative intelligence. My attempt at their meanings – according to Peter! – is a hopeful way of putting their wisdom in the simplest form. Gus Speth paints a picture of the environmental world with an optimistic brush. It is Gus's hope, his optimism, and his leadership that I want to pass on to everyone who reads this book.

> Leaders should point us toward solutions to our problems.
>
> John W. Gardner, *On Leadership*

We have only one chance to change the world.

That one chance is based on ECONOMICOLOGY: the right balance between economics and ecology.

Peter M. Wege

CHAPTER 2

Huey D. Johnson and GREEN PLANS: Greenprint for Sustainability

> Green is not simply a new form of generating electric power, it is a few form of generating national power – period.
>
> Thomas L. Friedman
> *The World is Hot, Flat, and Crowded*

Another contemporary leader pointing us toward solutions to our environmental problems served as secretary of resources for California's governor Jerry Brown in 1977. That is when Huey D. Johnson initiated an environmental restoration program called "Investing for Prosperity." As a former executive with The Nature Conservancy, Johnson knew what he was doing.

Huey created a 100-year "Green Century" plan to improve California's productivity AND environmental quality – precisely what I call economicology. Indeed, Johnson's program succeeded because, rather than doing the obvious and starting with the environmentalists, he first went to corporations – IBM, Southern Pacific, Bank of America, and the labor unions.

As smart corporate executives and as workers, these California business people all saw the wisdom of long-term, comprehensive, integrated, and large-scale planning to restore the environment. Johnson went on to create an unstoppable collaboration by bringing together the various individual groups interested in the quality of air, agriculture, water, energy, forestry, and wildlife.

"When you get them all together, it's just like sending an avalanche through a tea party," Johnson is quoted as saying.

Out of Huey Johnson's early vision for Investing for Prosperity in California has evolved the Green Plan, now underway in three nations: The Netherlands is farthest along, New Zealand next, and Canada is working on its own Green Plan. The urgency for promoting such national and total environmental efforts is told in the statistics.

Tragically, in the years since Johnson began promoting a national plan to cover the environmental board rather than tackling one problem at a time, the planet has degraded. One-seventh of the Earth's cropland has been lost; the human population has doubled; humans have destroyed enough forest to cover the Eastern part of the United States; and we've driven a million species of plants and animals to extinction.

The Green Plan is based on economicology. It recognizes that, as Johnson puts it, "our social and economic well-being depend on a healthy environment." It also recognizes our stewardship obligations now and for our children into the seventh generation, as the Native Americans say. Johnson writes:

> We must manage our natural and physical
> environment in a sustainable fashion if we
> want to continue to meet our own needs
> and to allow future generations to meet theirs.

The cost of a Green Plan means that it has to be supported by the government. Yet in order to succeed, the government officials running the Green Plan must work closely with the private sector, including a mainstream constituency of citizens. When – not *if*, because we must do it – the United States develops a Green Plan for this country, cities and states will be running their own individualized versions. But all of them will have to adhere to the standards set by the federal government.

No single environmental agenda will run Green Plans, because each issue – from global warming to clean water – is part of the larger whole. It is holistic. And it turns out that each separate issue gains power from being part of the larger, holistic plan. Everyone supports everyone else's particular ecological passion.

For instance, between 1980 and 1990, the destructive emissions of sulfur dioxide, nitrogen oxides, phosphorus, nitrogen, and volatile organic compounds were reduced by 30 percent, greatly improving the air quality. But in lowering those toxic emissions, the Dutch also cleaned up the water and reduced the amount of carbon dioxide released into the air thus cutting down on global warming. Similarly, the Netherlands' successful 20 percent reduction of pesticides used in agriculture has not only cleaned up the soil, it has also freshened the waste water that flows into the Rhine River.

Another example demonstrating the interrelatedness of the Green Plan's approach to healing the environment is its innovative flooding program. The waters the Dutch drained in the 19th Century to create more farm land had two destructive effects: first, it lowered the small country's water table; second, it destroyed 60,000 acres of wetlands. By flooding the land originally under water, the Green Plan is restoring habitat, bringing back wildlife, and raising the level of this low-lying nation's water table.

The Netherlands' clean-up of contaminated soil has led to safer crops, cleaner runoff-water, and less greenhouse gas expelled into the air. And the country's plan to plant 99,000 acres of forest will save the energy now expended in importing wood. That many new trees will mean a major reduction in CO_2 released into the atmosphere as well as inviting the return of wildlife lost when the forest habitats were clear cut. As Huey Johnson writes, the Dutch people have taken heart from such a large-scale movement because they see their country is committed to preserving the environment in total.

The great American statesman Henry Clay could have been speaking for the Netherlands and its Green Plan when he wrote: *A nation's character is the sum of its splendid deeds that constitute one common patrimony – the nation's inheritance.* But Henry Clay was writing about his own country, the United States. I have to believe his words are prophetic.

I have to hope that as our country makes the ethical decisions to protect and preserve the environment, we will define our nation's legacy. For me, the inheritance Clay wrote about must reflect economicology. We must pass on to future generations a healthy ecology that is in balance with a profitable economy.

I understand Huey Johnson's serious fears when he writes,

> The destruction of the global environment is an enormous threat to our security as a nation and as a species. Our response to it must be as great as if we were preparing for a third world war – nothing less will do.

The good news is that we don't have to prepare for a war! We've done that far too often in our nation's history. I have said before, give me the money that has been spent in war and I will preserve every foot of land on the Earth!

We can all share Huey Johnson's optimism when he writes that with "the example of the pioneering green plan, nations can light a spark in those without hope."

In fact, I sent copies of The Green Plan to the governors of the eight Great Lakes states and the heads of government for the two Canadian provinces adjacent to the Lakes. I wrote them the following letter to accompany the books urging them to begin a green plan of their own.

> This book is my invitation and encouragement for you to consider adopting this "Green Plan" that has been so successful in the Netherlands. As your states' leaders, you would be doing two vital things for your constituents. You would be saving lives and boosting your economy by creating a whole new industry based on this process.

> Please let us know...if your state would consider this plan.... It is part of Healing the Waters – Great Lakes, a national coalition that is supporting proposed federal legislation to restore and protect the Great Lakes. The HOW-GL collaborators see Johnson's Green Plan as part of the long-term solution for the Great Lakes states and Canadian provinces to follow.

> Johnson's book could create a new recycling industry in your state as the Netherlands now recycle 64 percent of its trash...(planning to) raise that recycling percentage to 95 percent.

> Huey Johnson's book explains The Green Plan in detail, and it could be a model for the eight Healing the Waters states and two Canadian provinces.

I urged the governors to read all of Huey Johnson's Green Plan as he describes how it works in the Netherlands. It is called the Dutch National Environmental Policy Plan (NEPP), and Johnson says it functions as a "guiding framework for actual improvement of the environment." Since it was introduced in 1989, NEPP continues toward its goal of full environmental recovery in 25 years: 2014. Through economic downturns and sometimes imperfect results, the Dutch have not wavered in their commitment to NEPP.

Johnson writes about NEPP:

> It is so accepted, so unquestioned in its central approach as to have become part of their value system, their standard behavior. They know it will only happen if everybody participates and so they've made it a 'social contract.'

In other words, the Dutch people, the private corporations, and the government are working as one to totally restore their nation's environmental health by 2014. Johnson makes it clear that the comprehensiveness of NEPP is what makes it work. He explains:

> The comprehensive nature of the Dutch plan is the result of careful thought by hundreds of the country's brightest people who have managed for the first time ever to put complex, interrelated natural systems into a manageable context.

And I would add, the Dutch had the guts to do it. Our country now has an administration in Washington D.C. with the same guts!

As with economicology, NEPP brings together the ecologies of water, air, soil, and energy, weaving them in with economics, health, and carrying capacity. The Netherlands leaders have allotted billions of guilders to making NEPP work. Johnson writes that the term "green plan means the whole spectrum of environmental issues is managed together so as to avoid partial solutions."

The green plan specifies both medium- and short-term emission targets. It then identifies the quantity of emissions that varying sectors of the economy contribute to the total number. Once those specific targets and individual sectors are spelled out, the government allows each industry to meet those targets by working out its own plan for reducing their emissions. Because they make their own plan to reduce emissions, the private sector can budget ahead for the costs of accomplishing this.

As Huey Johnson explains:

> In creating NEPP, the government wanted to tailor its policies to those social sectors that contributed the most to...(environmental damage). It therefore selected a set of target groups, most of which are composed in industries in various sectors that were very carefully chosen on the basis of the (negative) contributions they make...

The final target groups were agriculture, traffic and transport, industry, the energy sector, building trades, consumers, retail trade, environmental trade (water suppliers/waste sector), research and education, and public organizations. Once they agreed on these categories, the Dutch government further broke the target groups down into specific industries as some businesses clearly do more environmental harm than others.

For instance, they separated out the basic metals industry, the packing businesses, and the printing industry. Johnson explains: *The government has set both general and specific goals for these groups.*

And while the government's long-term goals for each of their target groups are "not negotiable," as Johnson writes, how they achieve them is wide open to discussion:

> The long-term perspective is important in this process of cooperation (between the private sector and the Dutch government), because it gives industry time to adjust.... But if you tell it where it needs to be (by a certain year), there is then room for negotiation and compromise regarding the short-term actions needed to accomplish those goals.

The old way – with regulations imposed from the Dutch government's leaders down – cost businesses more money and created conflict between the private sector and government. But because the Green Plan begins with an agreement between government and industry on both goals and direction, businesses can focus on the objective and figure out their own ways of getting there. The Dutch call this "a thousand shades of green," meaning companies can be as creative as they want as long as they meet the end goal.

They also know that if they don't cooperate, the Dutch Government will revert to the old top-down regulation which is more disruptive and costly.

The Netherlands' 25-year time frame for environmental recovery is not a random number; it is the length of one generation. Their slogan that "each generation cleans up" is one their citizens understand and embrace. Our country must do the same.

In the mad rush to plunder the Earth of its dwindling non-renewable resources, the leaders of today's industrial world have forgotten to make room for future generations. The Green Plan needs to be this country's environmental plan of action. The time for change is not some nebulous future date, but NOW!

> Today we have to build meaning into our lives… through our commitments…keeping faith with the future, with our children, and our children's children; and keeping faith with the best of the past.
>
> John W. Gardner, *On Leadership*

We have only one world.
We have only one life.
Let's keep them both clean.

Peter M. Wege

CHAPTER 3

Crimes Against Nature

As the largest provider of energy in the USA, King
Coal is this nation's number-one polluter.

Robert F. Kennedy, Jr.

You'll notice I ended my first two chapters with quotes
from the late John W. Gardner. That's because he is my
environmental hero, and the intelligence and wisdom
I found in his books led me to create the word and the
philosophy of economicology.

In my first Economicology book, *ECONOMICOLOGY:
The Eleventh Commandment,* I wrote about how John
Gardner turned me into a lifelong environmentalist in
1967 when he was our country's Secretary of Health,
Education and Welfare. That's when Secretary Gardner's task force on the state of America's environment
published their findings after two years of research and
study. The title of that report, *A Strategy for a Livable Environment,* has been my environmental Bible ever since.

Reading that report changed my life. I'll never forget
what Secretary Gardner said to me when I met him
in person in the late sixties. We talked about the need
for action to save the environment while there was
still time. When I promised him I would do everything
in my power to help make that happen, he said three
words I've never forgotten. "Move, Wege, move!" And
I have tried my best to follow his command ever since.

Had this country paid attention to John Gardner and

the serious environmental warnings in that report 40 years ago, today our air, water, and land would be far cleaner and safer than they are. The sad part then was what happened to Gardner's factual report.

Special-interest groups turned on the political pressure and lobbied Congress not to pass any environmental legislation that would restrict their particular businesses. In spite of these powerful lobbyists, Congress managed to pass the monumental Clean Air Act and the Clean Water Act.

The terrible reality today is that the same kind of special-interest lobbying for the fossil-fuel energy industries continues even under President Barack Obama who is a committed environmental advocate. The well financed lobbyists for the coal, oil, and gas industries continue to fight environmental laws that can help control pollution.

We now have 3,000 toxic chemicals spewing into the air every day. Big-energy's corporate leaders are growing rich while polluting our air and water. But their wallets are threatened by having to comply with anti-pollution regulations. So just as manufacturing lobbyists fought John Gardner's "Strategy" recommendations, so Big Energy goes on funding political candidates who will help minimize any environmental restrictions placed on their utilities.

In his 2005 book *Crimes Against Nature,* senior attorney for the Natural Resources Defense Council Robert F. Kennedy, Jr. wrote about what these big-energy lobbyists did to our environment. Kennedy noted that during George W. Bush's eight years in office, his corporate pals in the energy business were "Plundering the Country and Hijacking Our Democracy."

Kennedy's report on the coal-mining industry is his lead example. Kennedy's account makes it clear that for years, coal profits have overridden any concern for the environment. King Coal, as Kennedy calls it, produces more greenhouse gases and sends more

Robert F. Kennedy, Jr., photo courtesy of D&D Printing Company

mercury into the air and water than any other industry.

King Coal's disregard for the environment is matched by the industry's disdain for the public's health. In 2008, a research study by West Virginia University confirmed the obvious. Coal mining causes chronic diseases and unnecessary deaths.

Michael Hendryx, Ph.D. and Assistant Director of the West Virginia University Health Policy Research, conducted the study of 16,400 West Virginia residents in mining communities. The results showed a 70 percent increased risk for kidney disease and a

64 percent increased risk for chronic obstructive pulmonary disease (COPD). Dr. Michael Hendryx wrote his conclusions on how the health of residents living in coal-producing areas is affected:

> Total mortality rates are higher in coal-mining areas compared to the other areas of Appalachia and the nation. The incidence of mortality has been consistently higher in coal-mining areas for as long as Centers For Disease Control (CDC) rates are available, back to 1979.

That first tracking was done thirty years ago so this new study on the damaging affect of living around coal mining confirms what coal mining families getting kidney and lung disease have always known. It's dangerous to live in a coal mining town.

Dr. Hendryx confirms what his study has revealed. "Every year there are 313 excessive deaths in West Virginia among the coal-mining population."

But the health damages extend far beyond the mining towns themselves. As the largest provider of energy in the USA – forty-nine percent of our electricity comes from coal-fired utilities – King Coal is this nation's number-one polluter of the air all Americans breathe. In 2000, an EPA study done by the Clean Air Task Force determined that coal-fired plants cause 30,000 deaths a year. Between 2000 and 2006, the number of children treated for asthma in the coal-burning state of Kentucky had risen almost 50 percent.

Yet those numbers didn't stop coal-mining companies and coal-burning utilities from donating forty-one million dollars since 2000 to the political campaigns of anti-environmentalists. Those dollars proved to be well spent by King Coal when the Bush government rolled back New Source Review (NSR) standards mandated under the Clean Air Act.

The NSR standards required coal plants to install new technology that can control almost all the mercury emissions from power plants and meet the NSR standards. King Coal argued that the minimal cost of one percent of plant revenues to clean up their smokestacks was too burdensome. So far their profit motive has overpowered any concern they might have to the damage they're doing to public health and to the environment.

But with another 100 coal burning plants on the drawing boards during President Obama's first year in office, there is new economicology thinking at the federal level. Indeed, King Coal's very real fear that in the not too distant future there *will* be a costly cap or quota on the CO2 emissions they can put into the atmosphere has spurred them on to build fast! Today the coal industry is responsible for 30 percent of the total carbon emissions in the United States and 83 percent of carbon emissions within the energy industry.

Between 2000 and 2006, the number of children treated for asthma in the coal-burning state of Kentucky had risen almost 50 percent.

Big Coal's concern that the new environmentally intelligent administration will make them pay for those high carbon emissions has contributed to the surge in plans for more coal plants. The coal industry's leaders want to build while they can still put up the old and dirty carbon-intensive coal burners.

They want to get approved before they are regulated into using a technology that will spare the environment and provide energy, but will cost the coal industry approximately 20 percent more to build. The complicated name of the new green technology is integrated gasification combined cycle (IGCC). But the process itself is not so complicated.

In *Big Coal* by Jeff Goodell, who spent three years researching the coal industry's practices to write the book, Goodell describes how IGCC works.

> Instead of burning coal in a big steel box like conventional coal plants do, IGCC plants use heat and pressure to cook off the impurities in coal and convert it into a synthetic gas; the gas is then captured and burned in a turbine.

The author enumerates the advantages of IGCC over the old-fashioned dirty coal burner. The pluses of IGCC plants can't be refuted.

- They are 10 percent more efficient and use 40 percent less water.
- They create half as much ash and solid waste and are nearly as clean burning as natural gas plants are.
- Most important for global warming that threatens our Earth, it is easier and cheaper to capture CO_2 from coal at an IGCC plant than from the older coal plants.

How best to store this carbon is still a debate with no firm testing on what works. But in one sentence, Jeff Goodell summarizes why the United States must move forward with IGCC technology to replace the dirty coal burners now polluting the air across the United States:

> But the combination of IGCC with CO_2 capture and storage at least offers a plausible way to continue using coal without willfully trashing the climate.

My friend and fellow environmentalist Mayor Richard Daley of Chicago could well lead the way toward implementing IGCC in his coal-rich state. Mayor Daley is already known for pushing renewable energy, planting green roofs, and supporting our Great Lakes initiative to restore the five Lakes. Because coal is to Illinois what oil is to Texas, there will always be working coal plants there. But Mayor Daley's long-term environmental vision indicates he will spearhead his state's movement away from what the author calls its "rust belt image" and toward the innovative green technology of IGCC.

In writing *Crimes Against Nature,* senior attorney for the Natural Resources Defense Council Robert F. Kennedy, Jr. helped set the stage for forcing coal companies to invest in the IGCC technology that will clean up dirty coal. Kennedy's book was an early whistle-blowing on what Big Energy lobbyists were costing the environment. He was one of the first to document that King Coal produces more greenhouse gases and sends more mercury into the air and water than any other industry.

An article titled "The Rape of Appalachia" by Michael Shnayerson in *Vanity Fair Magazine,* May 2006, reinforced Kennedy's charges. The magazine's research showed that from 1985 to 2001, 400,000 acres of rich and diverse forest in Appalachia was destroyed by mountaintop coal mining. Researchers estimate another 100,000 more acres were cut down by 2006.

Some 1,200 miles of valley streams once fished by the people of the area are now polluted with mining waste, the toxic chemicals having turned them black. The people of Appalachia have tolerated this mass destruction of their woods and streams because they are usually too poor and too financially dependent and too afraid to protest.

Among the permanent damage that coal mining wreaks on the environmental landscape, perhaps none is more horrific than mountaintop mining. In his book *Lost Mountain,* journalist and Kentucky native Erik Reece, described what he saw the first time he flew over a mountaintop coal mine:

> All I could see below me was a long gray flat-land, pocked with darker craters and black ponds filled with coal slurry...the desolation went on for miles.... A vast circuitry of haul roads wound through the rubble. It looked as if someone had tried to plot a highway system on the moon.

The mountaintop devastation starts with clear-cutting ridgetop forests where families in the hollow have hunted, fished, and hiked for generations. The coal companies follow up that destruction of the trees by igniting three million pounds of explosives every day wiping out several ridge tops a week.

These detonations are caused by ANFO: a mix of ammonium nitrate and fuel oil that cracks walls and foundations, destroys wells, and pollutes the air. Erik Reece noted that this is the same explosive formula Timothy McVeigh used to blow up the federal building in Oklahoma City.

The coal companies' final act of destruction is covering everything in sight with dirty coal dust that spews from the open trucks barreling up and down the mountain.

Like Kennedy, Michael Shnayerson blames the environmental wreckage on money and politics. There are almost 100 new coal-fired power plants in various planning stages in this country – hundreds more in China – despite the fact that every year more people are dying from coal dust-related respiratory disease.

And the business interests looking to profit from those 100 new coal-fired power plants are apparently indifferent to the fact that poisonous mercury in those emissions settles in waterways where it's consumed by fish that get eaten by humans. Scientists know that mercury, even in microscopic amounts, is toxic to the brain.

Medical research also has shown that pregnant women eating mercury-tainted fish are more apt to have a baby with birth defects. Recent studies estimate that one out of every six American women carry unsafe levels of mercury, meaning 630,000 newborns are at risk for brain damage, blindness, and possibly autism (which is on the rise for no explainable reason).

Doctors know that for adults, mercury in the blood stream can lead to diseased kidneys, hearts, and livers.

People get contaminated with mercury mainly by eating fish. Most mercury in fish comes from coal-tainted rain and snow that fall into rivers and lakes. According to the EPA, coal-burning power plants account for 40 percent of the airborne mercury in the United States.

Most mercury in fish comes from coal-tainted rain and snow that fall into rivers and lakes.

I would think, and I'm no mathematician, that this process should have been tried before they destroyed thousands of acres of pristine land. The federal government could have insisted by law that this environmentally friendly process had to be used. But the political favoritism got in the way.

What the decision makers in the coal industry don't understand is that good profit and a healthy environment are inseparable: you can't have one without the other. I wrote *ECONOMICOLOGY, The Eleventh Commandment* in the middle 90s to inform students, parents, and citizens of the world that by protecting our air and water, we are protecting the economy and the health of all our citizens. My readers got the message.

Now, in this second book, I am attempting to penetrate the minds of the uninformed people who still don't understand that clean air and clean water are essential for our survival as a civilization. These uninformed people are the ones Robert F. Kennedy, Jr. and Michael Shnayerson are trying to reach.

In order to penetrate their minds, we must all get together as a team to educate everyone on the connection between clean air and water and good human health. When everyone understands this, the public will pressure the coal industry's polluters to end mountaintop mining and save lives in the process. The public needs to push the coal industry to reduce its dirty and deadly plant emissions by installing the cleanest available technology.

It's a matter of ethics, morality, and economics. It's unethical for anyone to do what the coal industry does daily: knowingly damage another human being's health. We can provide energy in a safe and humane way that does not sacrifice Economics. What I called the Six Es in my first book all work together – Ecology, Economics, Environment, Education, Ethics, and Empathy. Pull a strand of one, and you can have a positive affect on the other five. These Six Es are all about man's ability to understand the essence of the relationship between planet Earth and human life.

> We have forgotten how to be good guests, how to walk lightly on the earth as other creatures do.
>
> 1972 *Only One Earth Conference*

Reeds Lake in East Grand Rapids, Michigan, photo taken by Peter M. Wege

CHAPTER 4

Healing Our Waters:
Saving the Great Great Lakes

The Great Lakes have enriched my life as
they have so many others, and I share your
commitment to restoring them for our children's
and grandchildren's future.

President Gerald R. Ford
In a letter to Peter M. Wege July 26, 2006

In the fall of 2004, I wrote an essay that was
published in the October 9, 2004, edition of the
Grand Rapids Press. The headline summarized my
subject: *Great Lakes Rescue Will Require Lifeline
From Government.* Just as Huey Johnson documents
in his book *Green Plans,* the environmental solutions
we must have to save the planet are too big to be
done by any one institution smaller than the national
government. For the Great Lakes, that means the
federal government of the United States and the
governments of the two Canadian provinces in the
Great Lakes basin, Quebec and Ontario.

As I wrote in the Press essay to my fellow citizens
in Grand Rapids, Michigan, our magnificent Great
Lakes are under siege. Containing over 95 percent
of America's surface fresh water, the Lakes sustain
millions of people and diverse natural wildlife. The
Great Lakes are vital to the region's economy and
way of life, but we have contaminated the water and
fish. By allowing ships from foreign lands to dump
ballast water in the Great Lakes, we have introduced

July 26, 2006

GERALD R. FORD

Dear Peter:

Thank you for your letter updating me on the pending initiativ...
...Great Lakes and on the "Healing Our Waters Coalition" you fo...
...ppreciate the leadership you and the Wege Foundation are prov...
...ically important issue.

...you, with our shared roots in West Michigan, I understand the
...rnational importance of the Great Lakes. The Great Lakes su...
...s of eight states, provide drinking water for millions of peopl...
...recreational resource and, of course, are renown for their nat...
...Great Lakes have enriched my life as they have so many oth...
...ur commitment to restoring and protecting them for our
...randchildren's future.

...sion that restoring the Great Lakes must be a colla...
...rnments at all levels, businesses, and citiz...
...hat another long-time friend from...
...ts in Congress to bring ne...
...'s a great team...

non-native invasive species that are destroying the natural ecosystem.

Recognizing this dangerous reality, in the spring of 2004 I invited 70 of the nation's top scientists, non-profit leaders, and government officials to meet in Grand Rapids at Steelcase University. Out of that two-day working conference, the Healing Our Waters Great Lakes Coalition (HOW-GL) was created. Given that I was in my eighties at the time, I asked the group to collaborate on restoring the Lakes within five years.

These intelligent and experienced leaders blinked at the time frame: the speed of light for such an enormous task. But they woke up fast! Tom Kiernan, president of the National Parks Conservation Association, and Andy Buchsbaum, Director of the National Wildlife Federation Great Lakes Office, jumped in to organize and co-chair this gargantuan five-year effort. Mark Van Putten, former president of the National Wildlife Federation, came on board as my consultant to the coalition.

These wonderful young men and national leaders share my passion for the Great Lakes. Tom and Andy and Mark accepted my challenge and went to work. What they accomplished has been nothing short of miraculous. By September 2006, those original 70 guests who created the HOW-GL Coalition had grown to over 300 people who came to Cleveland that year for the second Healing Our Waters Conference.

And out of the 36 founding environmental groups who'd started out in Grand Rapids, within five years we had over 100 local, regional, and national organizations meeting in Duluth in September 2009. They were united in their shared mission. For these many good people who'd worked for years to protect the Great Lakes, this coalition was an answer to prayer. At last they could speak with one voice.

The representatives from the over 100 Great Lakes coalition members are fired up with the power of synergy and knowing that, at last, their treasured

President Gerald R. Ford's letter to Peter M. Wege, photo taken by Sherri Days

Great Lakes might finally have a chance. Their mission to inform the public has been clear from the beginning. First, they needed to get the word out to the 44 million people who live in the Great Lakes basin. Second, they needed to make sure Americans from the Pacific to the Atlantic began to realize that saving the Great Lakes was not a regional necessity, but a national and even global one.

The late President of the United States Gerard R. Ford, a native of my home town Grand Rapids, Michigan, said it perfectly in a letter he wrote to me in 2004:

> I understand the national and international importance of the Great Lakes…(they) sustain the economies of eight states, providing drinking water for millions of people, and are a wonderful recreation resource."

In the fall of 2004 following the original HOW conference, the coalition delivered to every member of Congress and a broad list of federal officials, policy makers, and environmental experts a report on what specific steps needed to be taken. These included three priorities:

- First, the federal government had to develop a Great Lakes restoration and protection strategy that can insure the waters are safe for drinking and swimming, the fish are safe to eat, native fish are healthy and reproducing, and the system supports a vibrant economy.
- Second, the federal government had to act as soon as possible to prevent the introduction of additional invasive species and remediate the damages caused by those already here. The coalition asked that the federal government establish liability for unauthorized introductions of invasive species. The HOW-GL further called on the federal government to authorize

prosecution of violators and provide adequate
funds to monitor and enforce the rules on
ballast water.

• Third, the government was asked to require and,
when necessary, pay for cleaning up the 31 areas
of concentrated toxic pollution in Great Lakes
river mouths and harbors that the government
itself had already designated as "international
areas of concern" way back in 1987.

To highlight this HOW-GL report, in late 2004 my
staff and I flew to Washington D.C. to host a reception
announcing its release. Our honored speaker was my
friend Michigan Congressman Vernon Ehlers, the only
person in Congress with a Ph.D in nuclear physics and
a Republican leader.

Great Lakes Day Coalition 2008, photo courtesy of the Healing Our Waters-Great Lakes Coalition,
Jordan Lubetkin photographer

Image by artist Mark Heckman

We knew the federal government had committed billions of taxpayer dollars to restoring Florida's Everglades. We also knew about the plans to restore both Louisiana's coastal region and Chesapeake Bay at the cost of many more billions of dollars. We all agreed that these vital ecological resources deserve the attention of the federal government and the United States Environmental Protection Agency.

But I say the Great Lakes deserve no less, especially given their global significance and the international and interstate nature of their environmental endangerment. As I wrote in the Grand Rapids Press essay,

> It is long past time for a comprehensive,
> coordinated Great Lakes restoration plan
> that is forcefully led by the federal government.

In late 2005, University of Michigan professor Donald Scavia, Ph. D. testified before a Congressional hearing on Great Lakes restoration. Dr. Scavia, along with other leading academicians, had just completed a study of the Great Lakes. Their findings were frightening, but irrefutable. Another 200 scientists across the United States and Canada soon endorsed

Dr. Scavia's conclusions.

The study's findings are not hysterical speculation, but scientific evidence. Huge sections of the Lakes' ecosystem are deteriorating more dramatically and faster than anyone thought. As Dr. Scavia told the Congressional hearing, "The problem with ecological tipping points is that you cannot be sure you have reached them until it is too late."

The great news is that three years later, an Illinois Senator named Barack Obama would campaign for our nation's highest office with the promise of federal support for the environment. His Inauguration as President of the United States in January 2009 launched a new era for the restoration of the Great Lakes.

Thanks to the new economicology President, there is great hope that, as Dr. Scavia warned us, it is not "too late" for our planet's richest natural resource of fresh water. But the battle is just beginning! As citizens in a democracy, we must continue to pressure our elected officials in Washington to act on behalf of the Great Lakes. If we do not, then all citizens, even those beyond the eight Great Lakes states, will share responsibility for the destruction of the world's only freshwater inland seas.

> We can live without a lot of things; fresh water isn't one of them.

> Peter M. Wege

CHAPTER 5

The United States and Canada: Partners for the Great Lakes

United States Environmental Protection Agency

Two important leaders in the Healing Our Waters-Great Lakes Coalition published an important book in 2005 titled *Evolution of the Great Lakes Water Quality Agreement*. Lee Botts, founder of the Lake Michigan Federation and a U.S. citizen, and Paul Muldoon, Executive Director of the Canadian Environmental Law Association and a Canadian citizen, represent the international nature and needs of the Great Lakes.

Their book documents the remarkable history of how these two North American nations have teamed up to protect their mutual natural resource. In fact, the Great Lakes Water Quality Agreement signed in 1972 was the first international agreement in the world to restore and protect an ecosystem that crosses international borders.

In his book *The Late, Great Lakes,* environmental historian William Ashworth writes about the events of the 1950s and 60s that led to this historic Agreement. Beginning in the mid-fifties, news reporters started writing articles about beach closings along the Great Lakes because raw sewage was found floating in the water. Niagara Falls began to stink of what Ashworth calls "fecal coliform bacteria."

Through the decade of the sixties, Lake Erie became so polluted that a huge section of the bottom waters became a lifeless desert with no oxygen. Along with the rest of my fellow Americans, I was getting madder every time I read another headline like, *Lake Erie is*

Dying. The general public was slowly finding out about the environmental damage happening to our beautiful Great Lakes.

It is no coincidence that I started The Wege Foundation in 1968 when the outrage over the pollution of the Great Lakes began to boil over. And it is not surprising that this family foundation's first mission was to help clean up West Michigan's water, air, and soil. While Lake Erie was the first and most endangered of the Great Lakes, the other four Lakes were in jeopardy as well, and my hometown of Grand Rapids is 40 miles from Lake Michigan.

Ashworth is clear on how critical the situation was. He writes :

> And make no mistake about it: We did almost destroy Lake Erie...we did very nearly kill it.

In addition to sewage in Lake Erie, Lake Michigan was being contaminated with industrial waste. Green Bay, Wisconsin, for instance, was poisoning the lake with effluent from the huge pulp and paper industries located there. One national leader who helped fire me up to get involved was Senator Gaylord Nelson from Wisconsin.

During heated U.S. Public Health Service hearings on Lake Erie, Senator Gaylord accused industries in Cleveland and along the Lake Erie shoreline of turning Erie "from a body of water into a chemical tank."

June 22, 1969, was the final straw when the Cuyahoga River caught on fire from the flammable industrial waste filling its waters. The author of *The Late, Great Lakes* writes that "the death of Lake Erie marked the birth of the modern environmental movement." The Wege Foundation was almost a year old and the first Earth Day happened the year after the Cuyahoga caught on fire.

The 1972 International Great Lakes Water Quality Agreement Botts and Muldoon write about was not the only leap forward in 1972. The first U.S. Clean Water Act also became law, requiring polluters to be penalized. The new legislation also offered federal funds to help Great Lakes communities upgrade their sewage treatment plants.

While both of those 1972 legal documents made historic environmental leaps forward, the significant feature of the Great Lakes Water Quality Agreement (GLWQA) was that it was international. Both President Nixon and Canadian Prime Minister Pierre Trudeau signed it.

These two North American nations committing to work as one marked a major turning point for protecting our shared Great Lakes. That Great Lakes Water Quality Agreement triggered vital legislation in both this country and Canada that made defending the Lakes a priority for both nations.

Since one-fourth of all Canadians live in the Great Lakes' province of Ontario, this 1972 treaty had a huge impact on all of Canada. The Agreement declared the lakes and their basins are a shared ecosystem being damaged by toxic pollutants. The Agreement stated that its objective is to "restore and maintain the chemical, physical, and biological integrity of the Great Lakes."

Botts and Muldoon, the American and the Canadian writers, make it clear that while earlier blame for the water pollution was directed at the industrial discharges and sewer overflows, by 1972 the scientists realized the damage was far more widespread. The pollution was coming directly from industry and sewer plants, to be sure. But it was also coming from non-point sources such as runoff phosphorus from the land and from what was known as "acid rain" or airborne pollution.

Botts and Muldoon confirmed Robert F. Kennedy, Jr.'s findings in *Crimes Against Nature:* the major air polluters in this country are the coal burners. And the toxins they spew into the air end up in Great Lakes waters.

In 1978 the GLWQA was updated in an important fashion. Scientists were able to convince the two nations that dealing with only the quality of the water was insufficient; they needed to take a more holistic approach. As Dr. J.R. Vallentyne, with the Canadian Department of Fisheries and Oceans at the Canada Center for Inland Waters put it at the time, the 'law' of ecology is that everything is interconnected.

Dr. Vallentyne called for an "ecosystem approach" that considered humans as part of the complex natural system that included air, water, land, and other living things. On November 22, 1978, the United States and Canada signed the updated version of the GLWQA with its holistic, ecosystem plan for protecting and healing the Great Lakes.

In their chronology of the GLWQA, Botts and Muldoon describe what happened to the promise of that 1978 holistic update. During the 1990s, the rise of conservative politics both in Canada and the United States elected leaders who were more interested in the economy than the environment. Of course any of these officials intelligent enough to understand economicology would know that neither nation can ever have an economy without a healthy ecology!

For Canada, it took a tragedy in 2001 to propel a swing from anti-green politics to pro-environment thinking. In the small town of Walkerton, Ontario, seven people died and over 2,000 got sick from E. coli contamination of drinking water. In October 2003, the conservative Premier who had cut spending to restore the Great Lakes lost his re-election race. The new Premier Dalton McGuinty committed himself to supporting regulations that would prevent another Walkerton from happening.

In the four years since United States citizen Lee Botts and Canadian citizen Paul Muldoon published their historical account *Evolution of the Great Lakes Water Quality Agreement,* the world of the Great Lakes has changed. The international cooperation these co-authors represent and the agreements they write about are even more firmly entrenched now.

The 1972 Great Lakes Water Quality Agreement made history as the first international agreement to heal and protect an ecosystem. But an even more important historic leap forward was about to happen.

Water is the life blood of Mother Earth.

Frank Ellawageshik
Odawa Indians Tribal Chairman

Reeds Lake, photo taken by Peter M. Wege

CHAPTER 6

Great Lakes Water Quality Agreement: Finally an Updating!

In its current form, the Great Lakes agreement
does not sufficiently address the needs of our
shared ecosystem.

U.S. Secretary of State Hillary Clinton
Niagara Falls New York, June 15, 2009

At a meeting of the International Joint Commission
in Traverse City, Michigan, in the fall of 2006, this
bi-national panel overseeing the Great Lakes Water
Quality Agreement (GLWQA) of 1972, revised in
1978, came to a startling conclusion. Rather than
revise the Agreement once again, the Canadians
and Americans recommended their respective
governments go back to the drawing board. They
urged their leaders on both sides of the border to
start all over again and write a new treaty to protect
the health of the Great Lakes water.

Herb Gray, the Canadian who co-chaired the
International Joint Commission, made it clear that
the historic environmental agreement between our
two countries had played a major role in protecting
the Great Lakes since it was signed 34 years ago. It
led to vital restrictions placed on some of the biggest
environmental threats, such as untreated sewage and
industrial toxic discharges.

But despite these positive results, the GLWQA
never resolved some major problems. For instance,
with no deadlines in place for cleaning up polluted

areas, many highly contaminated harbors and rivers still contain toxins. Furthermore, with no tools in place to force the American and Canadian governments to enforce the cleanups in a timely fashion, the Agreement is ineffective.

"If you look at the Agreement now," Gray told the media, "there are lots of objectives and they're worthwhile, but they're not linked with deadlines."

A further downside of the 1972/1978 Agreement is that in the decades since, scientists have identified new threats to the Great Lakes, including invasive species, habitat loss, climate change, and urban sprawl. "What was once judged far-sighted and robust enough to protect vulnerable populations of humans, fish, and wildlife," the Joint Commission's report stated, "is no longer sufficient."

Any new plan must have timelines for cleaning up pollution, and it must have yardsticks to measure progress. Above all, a new Agreement must hold the United States and two Canadian provinces accountable for enforcing the environmental regulations. The strategy of a new treaty must consider the whole ecosystem of the Great Lakes rather than one piece at a time. As recommended in the 1978 revisions, protecting the Lakes requires a plan that treats the biological integrity of all the waters and ecosystems. By dealing with the ecological interconnectedness of five Lakes, a new Agreement could accomplish what the old one failed to do.

"We're just saying there's more that has to be done," Grey summarized, "and it has to be done in an up-to-date manner."

As if they both had heard Herb Grey speak and had read the book by Lee Botts and Paul Muldoon, United States Secretary of State Hillary Clinton and Canada's Minister of Foreign Affairs Lawrence Cannon made new history on June 15, 2009. That morning on the Rainbow Bridge connecting their two countries, the two national leaders signed an international agreement to update and improve the Great Lakes Water Quality Agreement. Secretary of State Hillary Clinton and Canada's Minister of Foreign Affairs Lawrence Cannon symbolically met in the middle of Rainbow Bridge to announce their plans for modernizing the GLWQ Agreement.

While the original threat to the Lakes in 1972 was chiefly phosphorus overload, in 1978 it was toxins, and in 1987 it was contaminated groundwater and sediment. In 2009, the dangers also include invasive species and climate change. As Secretary Clinton told the media, "We have to update it to reflect new knowledge, new technologies, and, unfortunately, new threats."

Canada's representative Foreign Minister Lawrence Cannon summarized my whole philosophy of eco-nomicology in his statements to the press at the June 15, 2009, event. "These inland waters are the largest system of fresh surface water in the world, part of our natural heritage and the foundation for billions of dollars in trade, shipping, agriculture, recreation and other sectors." Indeed, the economy of the Great Lakes depends entirely on the health of the Lakes' ecology!

Finally, Minister Cannon spoke to my prayer that nations can peacefully work together for the good of the environment: "Joint stewardship of the environment is a cornerstone of the Canada-U.S. relationship. This aspect of our long history of collaboration will remain strong as we begin a second century of jointly managing our shared waters."

> I understand the national and international importance of the Great Lakes...(they) sustain the economies of eight states, provide drinking water for millions of people, and are a wonderful recreational resource...
>
> President Gerald R. Ford

CHAPTER 7

Victory for the Great Great Lakes

"The health of the people of Michigan, our economy, and our quality of life depend on the Great Lakes."

Michigan Governor Jennifer Granholm

In their 2005 book documenting the evolution of the Great Lakes Water Quality Agreement, authors Lee Botts and Paul Muldoon were among the first to publicly name invasive species as the single greatest threat to the Great Lakes water quality. The American Botts and his Canadian counterpart Muldoon labeled it "biological pollution." Over 150 alien species have now been found in the Great Lakes; Botts and Muldoon make it clear that these destructive new aquatic species came straight out of the ballast water discharged from foreign ships.

In 2009, my friend Jeff Alexander wrote a book titled *Pandora's Locks* that chronicles for the first time exactly when and how invasive species began their destruction of the Great Lakes fish and plant life. Alexander, an environmental journalist, names the opening of the St. Lawrence Seaway as the cause of this natural disaster to our Lakes.

Alexander writes about the fanfare that accompanied the opening in 1959 because the Seaway's locks were such an engineering feat. President Eisenhower and young Queen Elizabeth took the first ride through it

Ellen Satterlee, Executive Director of The Wege Foundation, Gary Fahnenstiel, research scientist with the Great Lakes Environmental Research Lab/NOAA, Terri McCarthy, Vice President of Programs for The Wege Foundation, and author Jeff Alexander, signing copies of *Pandora's Locks*, are pictured here at the 5th Annual Great Lakes Restoration Conference held in Duluth, Minnesota, in August 2009.

together in the royal yacht to symbolize the historic international accomplishment that allowed huge ocean ships to enter the Great Lakes for the first time.

Through all the celebrations, no one foresaw the biological destruction these foreign ships would cause the Great Lakes. But as Alexander's title suggests, opening the fresh-water Great Lakes to the ocean-water ballast from foreign ships was, indeed, comparable to the Greek myth. Pandora disobeyed Zeus by opening the forbidden box that released evil into the world. The St. Lawrence Seaway released ecological havoc into the Great Lakes.

In scientific detail, *Pandora's Locks* recounts how the zebra and quagga mussels, round goby, Eurasian Ruffe, and spiny water flea, among others, spread through the Lakes killing off the Great Lakes' native fish and plant life as they went. The damage they have done in 50 short years reads like a murder story with these alien species as the guilty perpetrators.

Jeff Alexander's book exposing the damage being done by the foreign ballast water is so important that I think some day environmental historians will look at *Pandora's Locks* as the *Silent Spring* of the Great Lakes – it's as readable as Rachel Carson's 1962 book on pesticides was. And *Pandora's Box* also shares the hard science Carson researched for *Silent Spring.* At the time, Carson had to fight the chemical industry. Now Jeff Alexander has to fight the shipping interests and the Coast Guard who protects them. But Carson ended up saving the birds, and Alexander could end up saving the Great Lakes from its DDT in the form of invasive species.

My friend and Great Lakes expert Gary Fahnenstiel, research scientist with the Great Lakes Environmental Research Lab/NOAA, agrees with Lee Botts, Paul Muldoon, and Jeff Alexander that invasive species are the single biggest threat to the Great Lakes. But Fahnenstiel also expands the problem beyond "foreign ballast water." In a letter he wrote me in 2006, Gary said that we've been so focused on ballast water, we have overlooked the danger in other water coming into the Lakes including grey water, trim water, and wash water. Gary calls the "real threat" to our Lakes "the import of non-sterilized water into the Great Lakes."

Fahnenstiel, Botts, Muldoon, and Alexander are far from the only ones to identify imported water as the Great Lakes' worst enemy. Fahnenstiel has written and spoken about the fact that the scientific community at large sees foreign ballast water as the most destructive danger to the ecology of the Great Lakes.

Gary's letter said,

> I am not interested in destroying the shipping industry, rather I am interested in solving the #1

threat to the Great Lakes...we can have a vibrant shipping industry and a healthy Great Lakes. As you, Peter, have demonstrated many times, a healthy ecosystem can exist with a sustainable economy.

But the fear is that the Great Lakes ecology could become too compromised to support the Great Lakes economy! Getting the public to understand the deadly threat posed by invasive species has been hindered by the clearer water that swimmers and boaters see in the five Great Lakes. To their eyes this water is cleaner because it doesn't have weeds and green plants annoying their feet and floating on the surface.

It's a hard sell to convince the public that the Great Lakes are clear because the foreign species like zebra mussels have eaten the algae and plankton they didn't like swimming in. What many see as weeds are also the food our Great Lakes fish need to survive! Our Great Lakes have been ecologically depleted by invasive species, but the boaters, swimmers, and politicians don't seem to understand that. The blue-green water is so pretty – they can see so far down – it has to be healthy!

The past federal administration did little to help educate the public about what's important to the environment, including threats to the Great Lakes. As Gus Speth pointed out in *Red Sky at Morning,* one of President George W. Bush's first acts after taking office in 2001 was to reject the Kyoto treaty on climate change. By 2004, Bush's administration had rolled back more than 200 major environmental laws. This lack of intelligent vision by President Bush diminished the rules our country had worked hard to put in place over many years in order to protect our air, water, public lands, and wildlife. Over Bush's eight years in the White House, the alien species in the Great Lakes had plenty of time to multiply and destroy as they moved.

Yet I have always believed that mainstream Americans care deeply about the environment and they didn't support the last President's anti-environmental actions. This was proved in the 2004 elections when Congressional candidates running for office began hearing from their environmentally inclined constituents back home. What people in their home districts told them about their concerns for the environment made the Congress more receptive to our appeal for Great Lakes funding.

This political shift toward more green voters put our plans to heal the Great Lakes high on Washington's radar screen. In 2003, the House's Great Lakes Restoration Financing Act called for a new and "comprehensive Great Lakes management plan;" on the Senate side of Congress came a bill creating a Federal Coordinating Council. Both proposals included Canadian representation.

...no one foresaw the biological destruction these foreign ships would cause...

The various Great Lakes environmental advocacy groups were working out a strategy of their own to lobby for passage of the restoration legislation. Since I consider restoring the Great Lakes the most important single thing I have aspired to do since starting The Wege Foundation in 1968, I supported launching a new citizens' movement to restore the Great Lakes.

In 2004, after the Healing Our Waters-Great Lakes movement started in Grand Rapids, we joined forces with other Great Lakes advocacy groups already in place. Together we created the HOW-Great Lakes Coalition. Mark Van Putten, past president of the National Wildlife Federation, helped organize this Coalition of many groups with the one common cause of restoring the Lakes.

A significant difference between our HOW-GL

Coalition and earlier Great Lakes advocacy organizations is that previously they focused primarily within the watershed. Our HOW Coalition's aim was to build a Pacific-to-Atlantic constituency for the Great Lakes as a national, rather than regional, treasure as well as an international resource shared directly with Canada. The plan we developed in Grand Rapids in 2004 became the basis for the federal-state Great Lakes restoration plan completed in 2005 and now being turned into action.

The Great Lakes community caught the spirit and all eight governors and two Canadian premiers quickly signed a letter supporting comprehensive Great Lakes restoration. A new Great Lakes and St. Lawrence Cities Initiative, organized by Chicago's Mayor Richard M. Daley and other Great Lakes mayors, quickly got involved. Mayor Daley created the Great Lakes Cities Initiative to energize activists on the Great Lakes.

Mayor Daley also wanted to fire up local governments by increasing membership in the association of Mayors of the Great Lakes and the St. Lawrence Seaway. Daley said his aim was "to get local governments to the table for Great Lakes decisions." Before long, Mayor Daley's new GLSL Cities Initiative had launched a best practices format for cities and was busy lobbying for the Great Lakes restoration legislation. And my friend and Congressman Dr. Vern Ehlers did exactly what he'd promise when we visited him in Washington in September 2004.

Congressman Ehlers collected 41 other Great Lakes Congressmen to co-sponsor a twenty billion dollar package of proposed laws called the Great Lakes Regional Collaboration Implementation Act. Seven United States Senators sponsored comparable legislation.

Congressman Ehlers followed that up in 2005 and 2006 by scheduling Congressional hearings where the HOW-GL coalition presented their case for passing the legislation that would address the very problems laid out by our original Healing Our Waters conference: stop the introduction of invasive species; prevent sewage contamination and toxic pollution; restore wildlife habitat.

As Lee Botts and Paul Muldoon point out in their book on the Great Lakes Water Quality Agreement, about 60 percent of America's steel and 20 percent of its manufactured goods come out of the Great Lakes area. Some 7,500-cubic-feet-a-second of water comes from the Great Lakes to provide drinking water for 25 million people. The Great Lakes have over 10,000 miles of shoreline and almost 4 million registered boats, one-third of the country's total.

In March 2008, I wrote Michigan Senator Carl Levin expressing similar recognition of the Great Lakes' economic impact on the 46 million residents living in the Great Lakes Basin. I shared the 2007 Brookings Institution report that projects the proposed $20 billion to clean up the Lakes will offer a financial return between $80 billion and $110 billion. That amounts to a return on investment of between three and four dollars for every dollar spent. Now that is economicology indeed!

I also wrote Senators Debbie Stabenow and Carl Levin that not taking care of the Lakes wastes precious taxpayer dollars. The Great Lakes Regional Collaborative Strategy estimates that invasive species are costing the Great Lakes region more than $5 billion a year.

So whether we're talking about the national economy's use of the Great Lakes, the health of the residents who live there, or the recreational opportunities the Lakes provide for all Americans, the answer is the same: they are one of this country's most valuable natural resources. Fortunately a senator from Chicago understood this. In 2008, President Barack Obama campaigned with a promise of federal support for the restoration of the Great Lakes, including $5 billion to finance the cleanup. He didn't wait long to keep his word.

In his first month as President of the United States in early 2009, Obama proposed $475 million in his first budget for Great Lakes restoration, including help for cleaning and protecting the Great Lakes from further invasions of foreign species in ballast water. Nine months later, on October 30, 2009, President Obama signed that $475 million expenditure into law. This means the federal government has made a significant "down payment" toward the overall cost of $20 billion for Great Lakes restoration.

I have called restoring the Great Lakes
my most important mission...

It's hard to find the words to express what this means to me as I approach my 90th birthday. I have called restoring the Great Lakes my most important mission since I created The Wege Foundation over 40 years ago. Our first HOW meeting at Steelcase in 2004 really pushed this initiative into fast motion! When I told our wonderful HOW team that day I wanted the Great Lakes restored within five years so I'd be here to celebrate it, I'm not sure they thought this was possible.

Nothing, they warned me, so big could move that fast in Washington D.C. But they said they'd try. And they sure did! With the help of every single person involved with the Great Lakes Coalition, they have given me the best gift of my life.

Wisconsin Congressman Dave Obey, chairman of the House Appropriations Committee, shepherded this "down payment" bill through Congress. Congressman Obey told the press, "Up until now, the approach to cleaning up the Great Lakes has been piecemeal. Now we have a plan that uses the best possible science to comprehensively address the main problems that threaten the health and economy of the Great Lakes."

Talk about economicology! Obey went on to note that the Great Lakes are the second largest economy in the world with over $200 billion of economic activity a year from manufacturing, agriculture, and shipping. Another $2.35 billion a year comes from the 911,000 recreational boaters who enjoy our Great Lakes every year and spend another $1.44 billion on equipment and supplies. Great Lakes recreation alone creates 60,000 jobs! One of every three Americans lives in the Great Lakes Region, which is home to 19 of the world's best research universities.

When Michigan's Governor Jennifer Granholm wrote me in March of 2009 thanking me for "your passion and support for the Great Lakes over the years," I had to set her straight. I assured her that it's been a collaborative effort from the day we first met. Without other passionate economicologists like Mark Van Putten, Andy Buchsbaum, and Tom Kiernen leading the way in Washington, we would not have the federal government committed to saving our Great Lakes.

Her letter acknowledges the economicology aspect of saving the lakes by noting that the lakes provide over 823,000 jobs in Michigan alone. As Governor Granholm wrote, "The health of the people of Michigan, our economy, and our quality of life depend on the Great Lakes."

I want to share the closing words in that letter from Governor Granholm – not just for me, but for all the millions of citizens across the land who have supported our HOW-Great Lakes Coalition:

> Thanks to your leadership and support, the Great Lakes have now entered the national political arena…. Thankfully, we now have a President committed to the support they deserve.
>
> Michigan Governor Jennifer Granholm

CHAPTER 8

Floods, Droughts, and Climate Change

The choice is ours: form a global partnership
to care for Earth and one another or risk the
destruction of ourselves and the diversity of
life. Fundamental changes are needed in our
values, institutions, and ways of living.

EARTH CHARTER Preamble

We are at the point in time where we have to stop
and think about what is happening to our civilization.
With the natural system reacting to global warming,
we have to change the way we live. In a book titled
Floods, Droughts, and Climate Change, Michael
Collier and Robert H. Webb document the damage
we humans have already caused in weather patterns.

Collier, a science writer, and Webb, a research
hydrologist, are with the U.S. Geological Survey. As
climatologists, these experts make it clear that natural
disasters like Katrina are not single events, but part of
a larger picture. They approach global warming from
the perspective of our planet's weather in terms of
wind, temperature, and precipitation.

In 1953, Charles Keeling of the California Institute
of Technology was the first one to recognize the
significance of the increasing amounts of carbon
dioxide in the atmosphere – the root cause of
global warming. The culprits weren't hard to find:
wholesale deforestation around the globe, widespread
industrialization, and burning of gas, oil, and coal. And

once these CO2 emissions are in the atmosphere, as much as 40 percent remains there for centuries.

These increasing concentrations of CO2 in the atmosphere raise the temperature of the globe because they absorb the sun's heat. When the sun's energy hits Earth, half the heat – necessary to life – is absorbed. But the other half of the sun's warm rays are supposed to return to space. Except they can't anymore. Now that man has emitted so much carbon dioxide into the atmosphere, not all the excess solar energy can escape as it once did.

What happens is that all the leveled forests and spewing smokestacks and overpopulation have created a barrier of carbon dioxide that the sun's excess energy can't penetrate as it tries to exit Earth, instead of returning to space as it once did, this excess heat hits the wall of CO2, gets stuck there, and thus over warms the planet. This is global warming.

As Collier and Webb write in their book *Floods, Droughts, and Climate Change:*

> You may be able personally to handle a degree here, another degree there, as the earth heats up. Perhaps it means breaking out the handkerchief and mopping your brow a few more times a day than before. But can the ice sheets of Antarctica and Greenland handle it?

The writers note that if the middle of the Earth heats up by two degrees centigrade, the temperature at the two poles will go up by 8-10 degrees C. Already Alaska's 100,000 glaciers are thinning. In the worst-case scenario, if Alaska's glaciers were to melt completely, the sea level would rise 3.0 cm. But the threat of the Antarctic's ice melting is far more frightening.

They write:

But if West Antarctic turns out to be unstable… world sea level would rise 8 m. Is there a threshold atmospheric or oceanic temperature at which this potentially unstable melting would be initiated? The people of Bangladesh, whose country is mostly at or near sea level, are very interested to know.

So would the residents of low-lying Florida like to know!

The United States Geological Survey, where these two scientists work, measures river levels, floods, and droughts. Their research is crucial because this information in necessary for meeting our country's daily demands for water. Because these scientists understand the interaction of oceans and atmosphere, they can do more than monitor water events. They are now able to see them coming.

"Will we use that knowledge wisely?" Collier and Webb ask.

Our history of interfering with nature's water supply doesn't indicate we will. In the early 1900s, for example, farmers and land speculators in Southern California saw water as a way to make money. They tapped the Colorado River near Yuma to feed irrigation projects in the Imperial Valley. But it turned out to be one of the wettest decades in the history of the Colorado. With the floor of the Imperial Valley 200 feet below sea level, "the Colorado knew a good thing when it saw one," as the writers of *Floods, Droughts, and Climate Change* relate:

The tap turned into torrent as the annual spring flood of 1905 breached the canal's head works. Within a year, the lower Imperial Valley, once dry, became today's Salton Sea. The Southern

Pacific Railroad spent the next two years dumping trainload after trainload of rock into the breach before finally forcing the river back into its southbound channel.

So why do we build dams and canals throughout the Colorado River drainage? Why do we mine groundwater under Tucson and Las Vegas? Why did we build 5,600 km. of levees along the Mississippi River – that failed during Katrina?

According to Collier and Webb:

> We invest in these massive projects as a form of insurance, allowing us to live a little closer to the river's edge, allowing a few more people to migrate to the desert, allowing a few more homes to crowd the gulf coastline. We build these projects based on cultural memories of floods and droughts.

Most Americans remember the much publicized and powerful El Nino of 1982-83 that created widespread climate abnormalities, The reason was that El Nino's warm water on the western side of South America heated up the surface waters of the Pacific Ocean. That unusual warmth caused the Pacific trade winds to lose their strength and reverse course.

It is no coincidence that in 1983, unexpectedly heavy spring rains forced runoff into the Colorado River. That made Lake Powell rise a 15 cm a day behind Glen Canyon Dam. The United States Bureau of Reclamation began releasing water from the lake, but could not keep up with the rising water. As a last ditch effort, they actually put plywood across the Glen Canyon Dam's spillways to keep Lake Powell from flooding over it. As the writers summarize that close call, "It worked, at least this time."

Collier and Webb go on to warn us:

> If we choose to be shortsighted, we can slap our
> newfound ability to decipher climate up against
> the wall of the future just like those plywood
> boards…. We can exploit these ideas to extend
> the effectiveness of dikes and dams right up to
> their breaking point…. We can adjust agricultural
> practices year by year to cope with drought in
> this time of global warming. We can employ
> long- and short-range forecasting to squeeze the
> last measure of protection of the flood-control
> systems upon which we have come to rely. We
> can continue to dump trainloads of boulders into
> our mistakes when the rivers run high.

Then the writers hit the root cause of global climate change that is disrupting the Earth's weather system. As the world's population continues to grow, the rhythm of flood and drought is transformed from a natural climatic pattern to a series of crises that threaten more people.

In 1998, these weather experts tell us, episodes of climate-caused floods and droughts were 50 percent higher than in any previous year. And as our population numbers continue to escalate, scientists like these two at the U.S. Geological Survey have to spend more and more of their time simply trying to avoid the weather disasters of floods and droughts.

In their conclusion, Michael Collier and Robert Webb offer this advice.

> Certainly we should continue to explore our new
> understanding of a globally connected climate
> and integrate that knowledge into the fabric of
> our lives. Certainly we should critically reevaluate
> the burning of fossil fuels, logging of rain forests,
> and other human activities that accelerate
> global warming…. The potential benefits of this
> knowledge are immense.

This is the only planet God gave us to live on. If we

continue to ignore what Earth needs to stay healthy, all of us are doomed. Education is our best hope. People must learn the facts about global warming and how it's disturbing weather around the globe leading to major disasters like floods and droughts. The "knowledge" is there. Now we must educate the public to use it before it's too late.

...disasters like Katrina are not single events, but part of a larger picture.

We are at the point in time where we have to stop and think about what is happening to our civilization. With the natural system reacting to global warming, we have to change the way we live. We must balance our economics with our ecology and reduce our population as soon as possible.

In his book, *Too Many People,* Lindsey Grant states that family planning is not just something we are entitled to practice independently. Rather, Grant writes, it is something the Earth itself needs to escape the damage of continued human population growth.

(Controlling population) is essential to the preservation of ecological balance in the face of a species grown far too successful.

Lindsey Grant, *Too Many People*

CHAPTER 9

The Fate of Man Revisited

> Never doubt that a small group of thoughtful,
> committed people can change the world; indeed,
> it is the only thing that ever has.
>
> Margaret Meade

One of my favorite environmental prophets is the British historian H.G. Wells. His book, *The Fate of Man,* is even more relevant in 2007 than it was when he wrote it in 1939. In my first ECONOMICOLOGY book, I wrote about Well's foresight in calling on mankind to think in global, rather than national, terms. His vision was for a World Brain that would transcend political borders and educate people on what had to be done if civilization is to survive.

Above all, Wells wrote that the idea and tradition of war had to be eliminated. Second, and what is not so clearly and widely conceded, is that the vast and violent wastage of natural resources in the hunt for private profit must be reversed. In its place, we must establish a collective economy for the entire world.

Third, Wells called for a world organization (now the United Nations) that must be active, progressive, imaginative, and exciting. One of the most profound statements in H.G. Wells' *The Fate of Man* was this tiny paragraph:

Nonetheless, it is only through the attainment of

a real world democracy that there is any hope for the ultimate survival of our species.

Wells was one of the first intellectuals to recognize the dangerous arrogance of human beings in thinking the Earth was created for them alone. In *The Fate of Man*, Wells wrote:

> There is no reason whatever to believe that the order of nature has any greater bias in favor of man than it had in favor of the ichthyosaur or the pterodactyl. In spite of all my disposition to a brave looking optimism...I see him being carried less and less intelligently and more and more rapidly, suffering as every ill-adapted creature must suffer... along the stream of fate to degradation, suffering and death.

Wells was right when he declared that the only hope for humanity is the "willful and strenuous adaptation" that will reeducate our species. "Adapt or perish," Wells warned us. Either man's will to live and his imagination will save Homo sapiens, or he will blunder, as Wells puts it:

> ...down the slopes of failure through a series of unhappy phases, in the wake of all the monster reptiles and beasts that have flourished and lorded it on the earth before him, to his ultimate extinction.

In *The Fate of Man*, Wells focuses on three themes, all interrelated. The first is that man's inventiveness and scientific genius have "completely altered the material environment of human life." Second, a surplus of "bored and unemployed young men...will probably shatter human life altogether."

Consider that Wells wrote that second prophecy 60 years before 9/11! The unemployed young men he had foreseen we now recognize as impoverished, young

Islamic terrorists blowing themselves up in order to massacre innocent people.

Finally, the way humans have organized society, we do not have sufficient means to adapt our way into survival. Wells knew that unless we raise the intelligence level where people worldwide understand our life-support system, the human species won't survive. I have worked for over forty years to improve the level of education, and I can't emphasize this point enough.

Wells wrote that until we do something about "this ignorance of ours, this universal blinkered ignorance, we shall be overwhelmed, we shall destroy one another." We see this happening in various parts of the world and we can do little about it until the intelligence level rises to meet this disaster.

But like my friend Gus Speth, H.G Wells never lost hope that man still had time to transform our universal ignorance into a global intelligence – his World Brain. And this British intellectual looked across the Atlantic Ocean toward our own country as the best chance to begin redesigning the way society around the world needs to be organized. Wells wrote:

> If only some small fraction of the still considerable wealth and energy of America could be turned not merely to a campaign against the ignorance of others but against its own far more dangerous ignorance; if only this absolute necessity for an organized World Brain, a gigantic but still possible super-university…set above (our current) but ineffective, scattered foundations…to consolidate them, if only that could fire the imagination of a few energetic spirits; then the whole outlook of the human species might still be changed.

With H.G. Wells' call for a "super university" as my guidepost, in early 1999, I called together the top environmental leaders from several major universities social sustainab[ility]

community
agement/
areness

Mandatory study abroad

to meet with The Wege Foundation and me in my home town of Grand Rapids, Michigan. For many years, I'd talked to anyone who would listen about the need for the best minds in our nation's universities and colleges to collaborate on solutions for saving civilization and our planet.

We titled that first "super university" meeting ECONOMICOLOGY and held it at Aquinas College, a small liberal-arts Catholic college. The excitement among the participants during that original meeting generated a commitment to gather annually in our shared vision for this super-university to help solve global environmental problems.

Over the following years, we have met in Ann Arbor, at the University of Michigan; in East Lansing at Michigan State University; in Houghton at Michigan Technological University; and in Grand Rapids at Grand Rapids Community College. From that original gathering of twenty participants representing eight colleges and universities, by ECONOMICOLOGY 2007, over 70 university and environmental leaders came representing 18 colleges and universities, once again, to Aquinas College.

And from the original eight colleges and universities, most of them in Michigan, in eight years we had grown to 18 including the University of California Santa Barbara, the University of Wyoming, Cape Eleuthera Island School/Institute in The Bahamas, Carnegie Mellon, and Yale University, among others.

In welcoming our roomful of high-powered academicians from some of our greatest universities to ECONOMICOLOGY 2007, I summarized what I knew to be true. I called them "the finest group of environmental scientists and thinkers and writers in the whole country."

One of our ECONOMICOLOGY speakers was Huey Johnson, whose Green Plan is discussed in the second chapter of this book. Johnson's optimism – what

Brainstorming board during May 2004 ECONOMICOLOGY Conference, at Steelcase, Inc., photo courtesy of the Photography Room he calls the "politics of hope" – echoes H. G. Wells' positive attitude. Yet Huey Johnson would also agree with Well's admonition, "There is no time to lose."

Our ECONOMICOLOGY members all recognize that sustainability must be the driving force of the 21st Century – we must learn to live with the natural system of the earth. This "super university" started in Grand Rapids in 1999 is determined to educate the public at large on how we can live within our Earth's finite natural resources. Now I hope to expand that concept to bring together leading colleges and universities of the world who will collaborate on educating all the people in their own countries about the necessity of sustaining, not draining, our planet's natural resources.

If our civilization is to survive, these education leaders must get this message through. As James Gustave Speth says, "however bad the situation looks, there are solutions."

> We need a World Brain, and to my insistence that the creation of a greater mental superstructure to reorient the mind of the world is an entirely practicable proposal...it is in America now that the clearest hope for a beginning of that World Brain resides.
>
> H.G. Wells, *The Fate of Man*, 1939

CHAPTER 10

E.O. Wilson: Harvard's Esteemed Professor, Writer, and Biologist

All the technology and computer systems in our world will not be enough to save civilization unless we have the wisdom and intelligence to use it for the right purposes.

Peter M. Wege

On October 20, 2003, I had the privilege of meeting and spending time with Edward O. Wilson, a Harvard professor, biologist, and author of over 20 books, two of which won Pulitzer Prizes. The occasion was a meeting of The Wege Foundation held at the Harvard Faculty Club in Cambridge, Massachusetts. Known as "The Father of Biodiversity," Professor Wilson spoke to our small delegation from Grand Rapids on issues of economicology, health, and world population.

Wilson summarized economicology in these words:

We will produce a better world by paying attention to a better market economy and to the natural economy. The natural economy is crucial to the market economy.

Professor Wilson confirmed what I have said and written for years. Because world leaders fail to see this connection between a thriving planet and a thriving economy, we don't pay enough attention to protecting and restoring the Earth we all need for life. The good news Dr. Wilson shared with us during a luncheon meeting at Harvard is that he knew of two top universities who do understand economicology and are doing something to promote it.

Harvard's Global Health brings together outstanding people in science and in business who are working collaboratively toward planetary health. The second university Dr. Wilson named is the Earth Institute at Columbia that actually advises developing countries on how to improve both their markets and their natural economies. Wilson sees this as the beginning of a trend.

A native of Alabama who has taught at Harvard for five decades, E.O. Wilson and I share the same opinion on the two major threats to our planet. Dr. Wilson said this to his guests from Michigan:

> Our world is facing the bottleneck of overpopulation and a rising rate of capital consumption. Our over-consumption is shown in our ecological footprint which calculates the amount of land used per person for food, water, government, waste, recreation. In the USA, it's 24 acres. Elsewhere on the globe it's 2.5 acres. If the whole world consumed what people in this country do, it would require four more Earths to support everyone.

In the face of these alarming numbers, Wilson offered a ray of hope by telling us that because women are increasingly better educated, global fertility rates are down. Women who are educated recognize that children from smaller families will be healthier and do better in life.

The world's birth rate has dropped from 6 to 3 per woman, and in Europe is below 2.1. World population will add another billion people to the planet – from 6.8 billion in 2008 to 7.5 billion by 2020, not that far away. Wilson noted that we'll have enough food, but water will be a problem. This is a good example of how the world's leading universities and colleges could make a critical impact by working together on the issue of water shortage.

In a letter to the Grand Rapids Press in 2006, I said the same thing. We must define an optimum population and learn how to contain it with family planning. Controlling our global population is central to any hope of an environmentally sustainable future.

We can't move too fast in educating and empowering the women living in Third World nations. By learning to limit the size of their families, these women will be doing the best thing for their own children as well as helping to save the environment. If we can reduce the world's population to a manageable size by getting people of all faiths working together, we can save the Planet.

The United Nations can be a starting point, but we must all agree on the common goal: survival of the human race. As I said in my first book, only when we are educated will we be able to make this goal happen. We *must* stem the tide of population growth or we will all go down in its final embrace.

In addition to our shared support for population control, Dr. E.O. Wilson and I are strong advocates for preserving rain forests. A University of Pennsylvania biology professor, and now a friend of mine, named Dr. Dan Janzen has worked with the Costa Rican government since 1990 to save that biodiverse country's rain forests. With the help of many others, we have managed to preserve thousands of acres in the rain forest. In addition to all the environmental

Dr. Dan Janzen,
photo courtesy of
The Wege Foundation

good these saved forest acres do, they also protect wildlife; giving animals and birds safe places to live and move around.

Dr. Janzen's work demonstrates what Professor Wilson talked to us about at Harvard. Indeed, Dr. E.O. Wilson cited Costa Rica as an example of what I call economicology. Let me repeat Dr. Wilson's exact words because they summarize what Dr. Janzen and his wife Winnie, a fellow biologist from the University of Pennsylvania, are doing in Costa Rica:

> We will produce a better world by paying attention to a better market economy and to the natural economy. The natural economy is crucial to the market economy.

Professor Wilson emphasized that over the long term, more money can be made in Costa Rica from harvesting plants to make medicines that can help prevent and treat diseases than from harvesting trees for lumber. That IS economicology!

In April 2009, I spent some time with one of Dr. Wilson's good friends and fellow scientists, Dr. Thomas E. Lovejoy who also "gets" economicology. Dr. Lovejoy is an internationally known biologist and founder of the popular PBS series Nature. The occasion for our conversation was the environmental lecture series I have sponsored at Aquinas College in Grand Rapids since 1996. Dr. Lovejoy spoke on "Climate Change: Prospects for Nature." Interestingly,

Dr. Thomas E. Lovejoy with Peter Wege, photo courtesy of The Wege Foundation

while his friend Dr. Wilson is referred to as the "father of biodiversity," Dr. Lovejoy is credited with being the first person to use the word "biodiversity."

Both these distinguished environmentalists recognize, and advocate for, the need to protect the amazingly diverse species of life on our Earth. They also both share my philosophy of economicology. In his Foreword to a book titled *Right Relationship, Building a Whole Earth Economy* by Peter G. Brown and Geoffrey Garver, Dr. Thomas E. Lovejoy actually explains the Greek roots of the two words I put together to coin "economicology."

Dr. Lovejoy:

> The heart of the problem (deteriorating global environment), in many senses, lies at the intersection of economics and ecology. Both words, as has been often pointed out, come from the same root, namely the Greek oecos, meaning house. Yet despite the best efforts of some very good economists and ecologists the two disciplines remain far apart without even a common vocabulary, and this lack of integration is a major factor in the downward spiral of the global environment.

This quote from Dr. Lovejoy is one more confirmation of economicology. Until we integrate the economy with the ecology, we can't make real environmental progress.

Both Dr. Lovejoy and Professor Wilson believe that the most important challenge to science in the future will be the need to explore biodiversity. For example, round worms are pervasive in the environment, yet scientists still don't know what round worms do! Of the 100 million bacteria, only 6,800 are known and named. When the necessary research on biodiversity is done, it will be on the scale of the human genome project.

In his many books, Dr. Wilson has explained how

understanding biodiversity will help us improve both science and medicine as well as develop new products. Learning the secrets of biodiversity will also show us how our eco system got put together. Why are there so many species of birds and bugs? What sustains them all? But, as Professor Wilson made clear, it will take a national effort to learn what we need to know about biodiversity. In other words, the world of nature needs our help in understanding how all the myriad species of life work together for a healthy Earth.

By learning how every individual species contributes to the health of the whole environment, we will see how we ourselves face extinction by our destructive ways.

Once we understand biodiversity and the vital functions of each species, we will realize the seriousness of losing any plant or animal forever. By learning how every individual species contributes to the health of the whole environment, we will see how we ourselves face extinction by our destructive ways. As Dr. E.O. Wilson puts it, "A society is defined not just by what it creates, but what it doesn't destroy."

In 2006, three years after several members of my staff and I met with Professor Wilson on the Harvard campus, he published a book directed at our nation's religious leaders. Dr. Wilson, a Harvard biologist and science professor for almost half a century, wrote *The Creation* urging church leaders to help "save the planet." Even though it's aimed at pastors, *The Creation* should be required reading for every American. *The Creation* is written as a letter to one hypothetical pastor.

Dr. Wilson, a native of Alabama, titled his opening chapter: *Letter to a Southern Baptist Pastor.* Dr. E.O. Wilson begin with a plea:

Pastor, we need your help. The Creation – living Nature – is in deep trouble.

Relating facts he knows as a Harvard scientist, Dr. Wilson warns his readers,

...if our destructive human activities continue at their present rates, half the species of plants and animals on Earth could be either gone or at least fated for early extinction...

Dr. Wilson knew that his minister readers might not understand why a Harvard biologist would "preach" to the religious community. So he explained he had decided to write this book to pastors because "religion and science are the two most powerful forces in the world today." Wilson holds out the hope that if "religion and science could be united on the common ground of biological conservation," the planet could still be saved. He is absolutely right on this point, and it is up to us to try and bring about that union.

For me, the most important chapter in *The Creation* is titled: *Exploration of a Little-Known Planet.* For two decades, I have told everyone who'd listen, "NASA, come back to Earth." E.O. Wilson reinforces my position that we are wasting money in space exploration when we still have so much to learn about our own planet!

Wilson writes:

Humanity doesn't need a moon base or a manned trip to Mars. We need an expedition to planet Earth, where probably fewer than 10 percent of the life forms are known to science, and fewer than one percent of those have been studied beyond a simple anatomical description and a few notes on natural history.

Professor Wilson says that biologists now agree we are facing the most massive extinctions in some 65 million years! And once this biodiversity is lost, evolution needs 10 million more years to restore it. Right now the numbers of known plants, animals, and microorganisms are estimated at between 1.5 and 1.8 million.

This great diversity of known species is impressive until we realize how many more forms of life exist that we don't yet know about. Scientists estimate that we have 3.6 million to 112 million more species we know nothing about. Dr. Thomas E. Lovejoy said in his lecture on climate change that we face the real possibility of driving 20 to 30 percent of all species into extinction.

Instead of NASA's spending billions to send astronauts into outer space, we need to redirect that money to fund biological researchers right here on Earth. These scientific professionals are educated to research the rich biodiversity of this planet. Using the billions in precious tax money to put a robot on Mars leaves very little money to pay our experts in biodiversity as they research how to protect life on our own planet – the one that keeps us alive.

Wilson writes:

> ...the amount spent on systematics in the United States, from all private and governmental sources was, in 2000, the last year an estimate was made, between 150 and 200 million dollars. That amount was distributed to about 3,000 systematists in this country, out of probably more than 500,000 professionals who can be classified as scientists of all disciplines. To say that humanity has been slow to explore the home planet is an understatement.

Wasting money looking for some kind of life in space does not make sense when those dollars could – and should – be used to discover what we have right here. The knowledge of Earth's biodiversity is crucial to our national security and to our very survival. What we do know is that the biodiversity of life on Earth is far larger than we ever thought.

Dr. Wilson thinks that what we know about existing biology today is less than one-millionth of what we will someday know. But just as we are beginning to recognize our planet has a biological richness we have yet to research, we seem bent on destroying it.

Professor Wilson writes:

> This diversity is disappearing at an accelerating rate, from habitat destruction, including habitat destruction now underway from climate warming, plus the spread of invasive species, pollution, and over-harvesting. If these human-caused forces are left unabated, we could lose as many as half the species of plants and animals on Earth by the end of the century.

As I have said and written about for decades, overpopulation is the chief cause of all the environmental degradation in our natural world. Unless we get educated enough to stop bringing too many people into the world, overpopulation will destroy life on Earth.

The vital importance of the rain forests that Dr. Wilson has long studied, and that I have tried to help preserve in Costa Rica, can be measured in numbers. While rain forests cover only some six percent of this planet's surface, they contain over half of the known plant and animal species.

In other words, the world's rain forests – about the size of the United States minus Alaska and Hawaii – are home to one out of two living plant and animal species that we know of. Certainly, there are many more unknown forms of life we have yet to discover.

Professor Wilson's book written to pastors ad-dresses the spiritual component of our rich, diverse environment. Most people care deeply about Nature, Wilson says. But they don't know why. Because they don't know why, they don't feel responsible for it. One reason, Dr. Wilson points out, is another issue I wrote about in my first book: the weakness of science education around the world.

But this global scientific ignorance about Nature can be amended. This is why Wilson addressed this book to "Dear Pastor." In the chapter *What Is Nature?* Professor Wilson brings biology and faith together: "If God seems unknowable," Wilson writes, "so too does most of the biosphere."

This Pulitzer-prize winning scientist writes that "Nature is not only an objective entity, but vital to our physical and spiritual well-being." Wilson approaches the religious community of this country from the perspective of a scientist. That is why he describes the process of evolution as "countless experiments."

> Earth is a laboratory wherein Nature (God, if you prefer, Pastor) has laid before us the results of countless experiments. She speaks to us; now let us listen.

Not only is there no conflict between religion and science, they are part of the same truth. All the questions of why we are here in the first place come back to scientific understanding and religious faith. Humanity needs both if we are to "Save Life on Earth," as Wilson's chapter title says. Indeed, they are the only forces that can.

I have said for years that in order to save the planet, the religious leaders of the world must come together and light the path. The leaders of the major religions must overcome their divisiveness and competitiveness if humanity is to survive. Professor Wilson understands that religions and governments must collaborate globally to educate all the people on how not to destroy our Earth.

The time is now.

If there is any moral precept shared by people of all beliefs, it is that we owe ourselves and future generations a beautiful, rich, and healthful environment.

E.O. Wilson

CHAPTER 11

Dr. Dan Janzen:
Biodiversity Researcher and Activist

While I have quoted E.O. Wilson and Thomas E.
Lovejoy, two internationally known biodiversity
scientists, I want my readers to also learn more
about my friend Dan Janzen. These three top
biologists have all known each other for over three
decades; E.O. remembers buying Janzen a Chinese
dinner back in 1964 when Dan was a starving grad
student at UC Berkeley!

These three leading scientists all share the same
mission of saving our planet's biodiversity. Edward
O. Wilson, known as the "Father of Biodiversity,"
recognized something special in Dan over Chinese
food forty-plus years ago. Wilson saw even then that
Dan Janzen was going to make a difference in the
world. "He was then as he is today," E.O. Wilson
wrote, "a wild man, highly entrepreneurial and
original. He charted his own course."

And he has charted his own course. Dr. Dan Janzen's
rain-forest restoration efforts in Costa Rica have made
environmental history. This scientist, along with his
wife and fellow biologist Dr. Winnie Hallwachs, have
helped make Costa Rica the most progressive country
on the planet in tropical conservation.

In the late 1980s, The Wege Foundation got involved
in its first and only out-of-country funding in Costa
Rica. At the time, Costa Rica's president Oscar Arias
and the Minister of Natural Resources Alvaro Umana
were launching a bold and innovative plan to protect

their nation's tropical environment before it was lost to ranching and lumbering.

I first heard about Dr. Janzen from President Arias and Minister Umana. They told me about two biology professors from the University of Pennsylvania who had come to Costa Rica for research but were now actively involved with the small country's conservation cause.

Dr. Dan Janzen and his wife Dr. Winnie Hallwachs had stepped partly out of the "ivory tower" in Pennsylvania to make a difference in Costa Rica. I was happy to collaborate with them and the Costa Rican government to begin buying small ranches and farms to be permanently preserved as national parkland.

In 1991, I invited Dr. Dan Janzen to speak at a Grand Rapids symposium on saving Costa Rican rain forests. We were all impressed with Dr. Janzen's environmental passion for conserving Costa Rica's threatened rain forest, cloud forest, and dry forests while there was still time to save them.

Peter M. Wege waves at the camera during a trip to Costa Rica, photo courtesy of The Wege Foundation

With help from many generous people besides The Wege Foundation, Dan and Winnie began piecing together small plots of dry forest to greatly increase the size of the western part of the Area de Conservacion Guanacaste (ACG) in northwestern Cost Rica. Over the next fifteen years, The Wege Foundation continued to help the two biologists and the government of Costa Rica put together land parcels in the ACG by buying them from private owners. Each new parcel became permanently preserved parkland in the ACG. And as global warming has intensified, this ACG expansion has grown to include more of the eastern rain forest as well.

From the first small purchases in 1990 through today, The Wege Foundation has supported Dr. Janzen's work but we are far from the only ones! I have always advocated collaboration, and the successful land preservation in the ACG is a perfect example. Over 8,500 other donors, including the country of Sweden, have expanded the ACG parcel by parcel. By 2009, the ACG had grown to 163,000 hectares (402,773 acres) from its original 10,000 hectares.

The bottom line is that today the ACG makes up a remarkable 12 percent of all Costa Rica's national parks, wildlife refuges, biological reserves, and untouchable forest preserves now in permanent conservation status. Perhaps even more impressive is that the ACG now encompasses as much as two percent of the entire country!

Thanks to the collaboration of the forward-thinking Costa Rican government, and the brilliant conservationist Dr. Janzen, the Area de Conservacion Guanacaste is the leading example of tropical forest restoration in the world. Proving its irreplaceable value, while the country of Costa Rica contains four percent of the Earth's biodiversity, the ACG on its own conserves 2.6 percent of the world's biodiversity. The ACG is also home to 235,000 species – as many

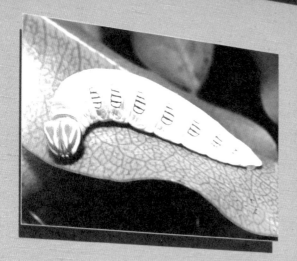

Porphyrogenes peterwegei

species as exist in all of North America!

Perhaps most significant for the future are the 2,500 Costa Rican fourth, fifth, and sixth graders who come to the ACG on eight different days every year to study biology and learn the connections of the forest and its biology to their own lives. While the cost for educating these young people is 20 percent of the ACG's budget, the experience is gaining the ACG permanent support in the future.

Dan and Winnie are grateful to every single donor who made this permanent conservation campaign happen. Dr. Janzen explains that governments have a tendency to provide funds primarily for researching and planning biodiversity conservation. But when it comes to actually *doing* the conservation, governments are not so eager to finance that necessary last step.

Dr. Janzen says, "This means we have to turn to generous and far-sighted people – of which, frankly, there are very few – for support of my actual conservation work."

While watching this happen has been all the reward I need, Dr. Janzen did something that deeply touched me. When Dr. Janzen discovered a new species of butterfly living in the ACG forest, it was the research biologist's right to designate the butterfly's name. I am humbled to write that the bright orange wings of this newly described butterfly will always be recognized in biology books by the scientific name of *Porphyrogenes peterwegei.*

And Dan Janzen went even further without my approval. In 2006, the first year of President Arias's anticipated new presidency, Dr. Janzen gave a permanent name to what was the Rincon Rainforest, a gorgeous piece of ACG rain forest covering 5,600 hectares (13,776) acres. That treasured forest was renamed for the two families who contributed the most to saving it. The name in Spanish will be Sector Stroud-Wege. In English, it's the Stroud-Wege Woods.

New butterfly species discovered in Costa Rica by research biologist and named *Porphyrogenes peterwegei* to honor Peter M. Wege, photo taken by Sherri Days

In his 2001 book *GREEN PHOENIX: Restoring the Tropical Forests of Guanacaste, Costa Rica,* environmental journalist William Allen writes about the collaboration it took to save the ACG. He recognizes the fact that saving the ACG required the contributions of many players in academia, government, philanthropy, and the environment.

But then the author quickly adds that my friend Dr. Dan Janzen was the lead quarterback. Allen writes:

> Although others played key roles in conceiving and executing the Guanacaste project, Janzen was by far its main character. The project simply would not have commenced without his ingenious and energetic articulation of it, without his daring push.

William Allen, however, is not the only one who understands what a difference Dr. Janzen's passion for biodiversity has meant to the planet. A lead article in the *Smithsonian Special Anniversary Issue* November 2005 titled "35 Who Made A Difference" named Dr. Dan Janzen as one of the world's 35 most significant people. Written by Jerry Adler of *Newsweek,* Adler quotes an earlier Smithsonian article from 1986 that called Dan Janzen "a theoretical Johnny Appleseed planting more ideas than a hundred other biologists."

Dan Janzen is far from done planting new ideas. His latest advocacy is described by Marguerite Holloway, science writer at Columbia University, in the magazine *Conservation in Practice: April-June 2006.* Holloway's article titled "Democratizing Taxonomy," wrote about Janzen's campaign to allow every person to be able to identify every living species on the planet.

Dr. Janzen's idea for accomplishing this began in the 1990s when a molecular geneticist – Professor Paul Hebert – at the University of Guelph in Ontario figured out how to get and index a snippet of DNA from a single gene common to all animals.

This gene, called CO1, could then be read as an

ID tag. Janzen recognized this new technology as a rapid, cheap and potentially personal way to identify a species from a specimen. This new biological scanner is what Dr.s Hebert and Janzen call "a barcode for biodiversity," as described in the October 2008 issue of *Scientific American* in an article by Mary Y. Stoeckle and Paul Hebert titled, "Barcode of Life."[1]

This new handheld personal pocket biodiversity scanner Dr. Janzen dreams of putting in the hands of seven billion people all over the world relies on the CO1 gene in the specimen to recognize the species. Right now the traditional way of identifying a species – classical taxonomy – is time consuming and costly. But worst of all, it as available to only a select few scientists! Standard taxonomy involves studying the structure, behavior, and genetics of the specimen in order to name the species, a tedious effort often taking months or a highly trained specialist – or both! Dr. Dan Janzen's bar coder can name the species within seconds.

Dr. Janzen thinks the 10 to 50 million species that are now estimated to live on our planet is probably too low a number. What troubles him about those numbers is that fewer than two million of all those living species have even been described. In Costa Rica alone, Dr. Janzen says there are 13,000 species of plants that require a different pair of genes to be barcoded.

It is understandable that in the science community of taxonomists, there is skepticism about Dr. Dan Janzen's easy-to-use barcoder. A vocal few taxonomists think the barcoder's technique of relying on the CO1 gene is too simplistic. While recognizing that the CO1 route also needs to incorporate traditional taxonomy, Dr. Janzen is sure the barcoder can work.

He wants to see what he calls "a barcoder for bio-diversity" that is portable and small and affordable for everyone. Dan Janzen refers to it as "democratizing" the knowledge of the natural world and its vast array of living species rather than confining it inside the biologists' laboratories and ivory towers.

Dr. Janzen says, "I want something I can stick in my pocket, and pull the leg off a beetle and stick it in and 30 seconds later out comes the scientific name, or else a light goes on and it says, this is a new species – and I want to do it for a penny."

Any person walking outdoors could take a bit of leaf or bark and insert it into a small barcoder, scan its barcode, get the species name, then Google the name and learn more about that organism. Dr. Janzen understands that only when people can identify what they are looking at in nature can they feel connected to it. If people can't name that species – and thus find out what humanity knows about it, they will have no investment in it.

Dr. Janzen writes:

> We have to move to what people DO care about, something that gives them a return. If you can't know what the objects are that are walking in your backyard or your house or your kitchen, or when you go into a park or to the ocean, then there is no reason to keep them.
>
> If there is a way of incorporating wild biodiversity into peoples' lives, it will be through knowing what it is. If you don't know what it is, you will destroy it. How are you ever going to get people to see the wild world as anything other than an object to be pushed away or chopped up unless they come to have some personal relationship with it?

Dr. Janzen calls his passion for DNA barcoding – coding the species to be read by his portable barcoder (all the millions of species on Earth) – a way *"to spread bioliteracy…"* Without this ability to name species, Janzen says, "People will go on treating nature the way you would if you were illiterate and saw a library as a big stack of thin sheets of firewood."

Dr. Janzen believes that we must be able to name a living thing if we are to care about it; only when we care about that species will we work to protect it.

> We are driven to find and describe our planet's unrecognized biodiversity because it is disappearing before our eyes, as well as because it is enormously useful to all of us.
>
> Dr. Dan Janzen

CHAPTER 12

Thomas Friedman on the New Global Economy

Together we must create a balance among economics, ecology, environment, education, ethics, and empathy. Together we must offer wisdom, love, and compassion for all our citizens.

Peter M. Wege, *EARTH CHARTER Commentary*

In 2005, New York Times columnist Thomas L. Friedman published a book titled *The World is Flat.* The book's name and theme come from Friedman's recognition that the rapid pace of globalization in the 21st Century is making the world smaller – or "flat." The huge investment in information technology that connected the world through the Internet happened at the end of the 20th Century.

At the same time, computers got cheaper and were sold all over the world. Added to all that technology have been the remarkable leaps in software – like email and Google. The result is the world has flattened out. These technological marvels have allowed information to be delivered anytime anywhere and instantly.

Countries once considered backward, like India, now compete for jobs everywhere in the world. That could never have happened before 2000. As one of Friedman's contacts in India put it, "The playing field is being leveled." The result of this flattening is that the United States economy has been hurt because our business leaders have not manufactured the products necessary for our survival, starting with cars that can get 100 miles to the gallon.

The new flat global economy Friedman writes about notes that outsourcing jobs to other countries has hurt American workers, especially in our state of Michigan. But he acknowledges that it is a business reality we must live with. Yet, like me, he sees the cup half full rather than half empty. Americans have historically done their best when challenged, whether by Nazi Germany or the Soviet Union. Competing for jobs in India and Mexico can result in a huge plus for the environment. But that will require economicology: we must find ways to balance the economies and the environments of the largest countries in the world.

To compete successfully in a flat world, American companies and their workers will have to become better educated.

Another major positive of this newly flattened world is that it requires more and better education. To compete successfully in a flat world, American companies and their workers will have to become better educated. Some of the traditional manufacturing jobs that required minimal schooling are gone. To earn a living, our workers will have to be better educated. And a more intelligent work force will also become a pool of environmentalists: better educated Americans will understand economicology. They will see that their own jobs depend on a healthy environment.

But the products we will produce must meet the test of economicology: they must help the economy and the ecology. The American automobile industry was slow in recognizing that small but quality cars must replace the Big Three's gas guzzling SUVs. These fuel-efficient smaller cars can attain the same speed but get up to 65 miles a gallon. We could have done this instead of letting the Japanese make all the hybrids first!

Our auto industry woefully misread the need for these high-mileage cars in their obsession with more profitable big cars and trucks. The result in 2009 is a bankrupt General Motors, something no one ever thought possible, and the sale of Chrysler to an Italian company named Fiat!

We now have to rethink what cars and consumer products are needed by our buying public. For sure, what we produce must be of the same high quality as what we are getting from Europe, India, Japan, and China. This can be done, but it requires paying a lower hourly wage and ending the obscenely huge salaries our corporate leaders have been earning. We accomplished this in the boom after World War II and we can do it again – only this time we won't pollute the air, water, and soil!

Better educated Americans will realize that the Earth's ecology is the life-support system keeping us alive and healthy. Education is the main hope for humanity in this new, flattened world. Only by raising the level of education will we be able to preserve and protect a livable environment so people around the world can lead full, productive lives.

Through more education, people worldwide will understand the interconnectedness of our life-support system. Citizens around the globe will see the direct links between good health and clean air, between good health and clean water. These more knowledgeable workers will see the world as a complex system we must understand if we are to survive.

Reading our daily papers and scanning our TV news, we will find that our intelligence level badly needs improving. We have a long way to go before mankind is educated enough to make sure the world offers a healthy quality of life for all. But the education required in this new, flat Earth can make the difference.

One of the greatest threats to the environment is the world's growing dependence on oil. Friedman notes that in Beijing alone – just one city in China – one thousand new gas-powered cars are put on the roads every single day! This is in a city already dirty with pollution.

In this new, flat world of instant information, people in India, China, Latin America, and the former Soviet Union now see for themselves on the Internet all the material goods they can't get and lifestyles they don't have. Through the worldwide web and mass media, they see the cars, houses, refrigerators, and microwaves the middle class in the more developed nations already have. They want the same things.

Remembering what E.O. Wilson said about over consumption in this country, imagine what the ecological footprint will be as these emerging nations demand the same consumer goods the rest of the world already has. Wilson defined an ecological footprint as the amount of land it takes to supply food, water, used waste, government, and recreation to support each person: 24 acres in the United States compared to 2.5 acres worldwide.

But with hugely populated countries like China and India demanding the same consumer goods, how long will it be before their 2.5 acres per person become our country's 24 acres each? Wilson speculated that if everyone in the world consumed as much as Americans do, it would require four more Earths to support all of us.

This means that all countries must have population control as soon as possible. Nations like China and India must bring their populations down to a level that their living areas can support. Overcrowding will be the demise of those countries if they don't mandate policies to contain population growth. Friedman projects what will happen as these emerging nations continue to overpopulate the planet while they go after their own "Great Dreams:"

> The Great Chinese Dream, like the Great Indian
> Dream, the Great Russian Dream, and the Great
> American Dream, is built around a high-energy,
> high-electricity, high-bent-metal lifestyle...the
> thirty thousand new cars a month in Beijing
> and the cloud of haze that envelops the city on
> so many days...testify to the environmental
> destruction that could arise...

Friedman writes that too many people consuming too many manufactured goods guarantees an environmental disaster will happen "if clean alternative renewable energies are not developed soon." We have no time to waste in getting our technological ingenuity to solve these problems!

Already sixteen of the twenty most polluted cities in the world are in China. If China's current growth trends continue, that country will go from importing seven million barrels of oil a day to 14 million by 2012. Friedman notes, "For the world to accommodate that increase, it would have to find another Saudi Arabia. This is not likely, which doesn't leave many good options." But among the options we do have are building more and faster rail systems, which is already being done outside the United States. It needs to be done here as well.

I think Friedman is right on target when he writes this in *The World Is Flat:*

> The only thing – and the best thing – we in
> the United States and Western Europe can
> do to nudge China toward (reducing energy
> consumption) is set an example by changing our
> own consumption patterns. That would give us
> some credibility to lecture others.

Friedman quotes leading oil economist Philip

Verleger who said, "Restoring our moral standing on energy is now a vital national security and environmental issue." Friedman goes on to say that we have demonstrated a kind of national immorality by consuming a disproportionate share of the world's oil. The consequence is that we have jeopardized our country's security by becoming dependent on oil from Middle East nations that do not wish us well. We must take the lead in converting to alternative energy if we are to regain the world's respect both for our ethical environmentalism and for our strength as a global leader.

Friedman accurately names solutions that have to start in Washington D.C. With an environmental President having replaced an anti-environmentalist, I have to believe the United States will supply more funds for alternative energy, seriously push conservation, levy a gas tax to force more consumers to buy hybrids and smaller cars, and pass laws forcing Corporate Average Fuel Economy (CAFE) standards on our auto makers, whatever companies end up surviving. The other piece of this is extending rail systems to more cities.

We have great problems in this country, and the sooner we face them, the better. Our leaders must look to the future, which is bleak unless we deal with the serious issue of energy. We must find a substitute for the gasoline engine that will free us from dependence on foreign oil.

I started this chapter on the positive note of my faith in the Six Es, and I am optimistic about the future. I am part of what Tom Brokaw calls "the greatest generation" who accomplished the impossible in World War II. In a few short years, our government converted our economy from a domestic one into the greatest weapons producer on the planet. We turned peaceful young men like myself into a military force that defeated the powerful war machines of Germany and Japan.

That liberation from the threat of Fascism came at great sacrifice, but we did it. Our reliance on Middle East oil is every bit as much a threat to our lives and liberty as Hitler's Nazis were. We have the ability and the will to free ourselves from the insanity of terrorism by ending our dependence on Middle East oil. We must balance our economics, ecology, and environment with education, ethics, and empathy. Together we can do this.

> The flat world has also been such a huge boon for al-Qaeda and its ilk because of the way it enables the small to act big, and the way it enables small acts – the killing of just a few people – to have big effects...the flat world makes it much easier for terrorists to transmit their terror.
>
> Thomas L. Friedman

CHAPTER 13

Natural Capitalism: Creating the Next Industrial Revolution

The environment is not a minor factor of
production but rather is an envelope containing,
provisioning, and sustaining the entire economy.

Paul Hawken and Amory and L. Hunter Lovins

If *Natural Capitalism* by Paul Hawken and Amory
and L. Hunter Lovins hadn't came out the year *after*
my first ECONOMICOLOGY book was published,
I would have included it. These three authors, one
an entrepreneur and the other two environmental
futurists, have collaborated on this visionary book.
The title names their thesis: a capitalist economy
based on nature must create the second industrial
revolution if we are going to save the planet.

The Industrial Revolution of the last two centuries
is over. This old system driven by market forces and
free enterprise can no longer determine the economy
if humanity is to survive. Beginning in the early 19th
Century, machines run by water, wood, charcoal, oil,
and later electricity allowed industries to massively
increase their production of goods. As the quantity of
manufactured goods went up, the costs to produce
them went down.

This first Industrial Revolution had a seemingly
endless supply of the natural resources needed to
produce goods. But what was harder to come by
in the 1800s and 1900s was a large enough source

of labor to make the products. Today it's just the opposite. We have an overpopulation – with 10,000 babies born every hour! – and too few jobs. And the Earth's once abundant supply of natural capital, such as wood and oil, has been depleted while the natural resources of water and air have been polluted.

Hawken and the Lovins tell us what must happen in this new industrial revolution if civilization is to survive. We must begin to organize our economy not around the old-fashioned system of supply and demand, but around what these writers call "the biological realities of nature." In this second Industrial Revolution, CPAs will have to place a cost value on natural capital as a limited, but necessary, factor in all production.

In the First Industrial Revolution, the private sector's goal was to improve human productivity. The radical switch we must now make for this Second Industrial Revolution is that instead of making *workers* more productive, we must now focus on increasing *resource* productivity. In other words, we must learn how to produce the same amount of goods and services we do now, but we must also learn how to use less material and less energy to accomplish that goal.

Forward-looking companies are already coming up with creative ways to make our natural capital of energy, metals, water, and forests work far harder than they do now. Increased resource efficiency means doing more with less. Until now, efficiency has always been measured in money. By investing in this new productivity revolution, we will not only save resources and improve the quality of life, but we will also end up paying back the initial costs.

Resource-efficient lighting helps us see better; fuel-efficient buildings are healthier and more comfortable. We will be better nourished by food that uses fewer natural resources to grow. I bought one of the first hybrid cars sold in this country: the Honda Insight. Since then, I have bought other hybrids made by

Ford and Toyota. By saving on fuel, steel, and rubber, among other things, these hybrids are an example of resource efficiency. They are the first wave of our automobile future. Fuel cells powered by hydrogen will be the next.

I didn't call it resource efficiency, but in my first ECONOMICOLOGY book, I wrote about this same principle when I explained humanity's need to find a balance between the environment and the economy. Since I started The Wege Foundation in 1967, I've collaborated with many others who understand economicology well enough to get this way of thinking into the mainstream.

This concept of balancing our ecology with our economy is spelled out by Hawken, Lovins, and Lovins. Chapters 8 and 9 of *Natural Capitalism* must be read to see the Big Picture. It's what I tried to convey in my first book and now in this one. But it takes a long time for the truth about our life-support system to reach every person on planet Earth. *Natural Capitalism* is sending that message.

If the intelligent world leaders of governments, major religions, and educational institutions fail to teach the facts about our natural system of life, then our current civilization will not survive. So let us proceed to learn from the great thinking of Paul Hawken, Amory, and Hunter Lovins. Let them help lead us to the knowledge of our natural life systems and the higher quality of life that will come from that understanding.

My thesis in this book, as it was in my first book, is that Education, Empathy, Ethics, Economy, Environment, and Ecology are the Six Es we must have to save this planet. One example of how we need to employ all six Es is demonstrated in the eighth chapter of *Natural Capitalism*.

Because fishermen are allowed to fish oceans with lines thirty miles long, every year we destroy 20 million tons of bycatch: dead or dying ensnared turtles, dolphins, swordfish, and marlin that had the bad luck to swim into thirty miles of fish nets. Where is the Ethics in that wasteful destruction of life?

Without raising the level of intelligence through education, we will go on killing off the world's fish as though the oceans had an eternal supply.

These unintended catches of sea life are tossed overboard without a second thought. Where is the Empathy for the starving poor who would love to have that discarded fish to fill their empty bellies? The quantity of this wasted sea life amounts to ten pounds of fish for everyone on Earth! Think how many families in Third World countries could feast on that fish instead of going to bed hungry every night.

Is it any wonder that most of the Earth's fisheries are being fished out and that one-third of all fish species are threatened with extinction? Without raising the level of intelligence through education, we will go on killing off the world's fish as though the oceans had an eternal supply.

Visible proofs of our destructive abuse of sea life are the dead zones on the planet that are getting bigger every day. The dead zone off the Louisiana coast is a direct result of the nitrate runoff from fertilizers along the Mississippi River. Our destructive habits have created this 7,000-square-mile dead zone where no marine life can live. It is ruining a fishing industry that used to bring in $26 billion a year.

It's pure Environmental and Ecological ruin; it damages the Economy; it's not Ethical to deprive future generations of safe fish and clean water; it shows no Empathy for fishing families, and it is plain stupid. It proves our lack of Education.

These authors said it exactly right when they wrote,

"If current trends continue, humanity will dramatically alter or destroy virtually all of Earth's remaining natural ecosystems within a few decades."

If anyone thinks we can somehow replace these ecosystems after we've destroyed them, they need to name the technology that can do it. I'd like to see how those uneducated people who refuse to see how we're ruining the planet would accomplish any single item from this list in *Natural Capitalism* that names the benefits Mother Nature does for us when we stay out of her way:

> produce oxygen; purify water and air; store and distribute fresh water around the globe; regulate the atmosphere's chemical makeup; decompose organic wastes; detoxify human/industrial waste; control soil erosion and sediment; prevent floods; regulate the ocean's chemistry; regulate climate; create topsoil and make it fertile.

Read that list again and see if you think the smartest inventors in the world could duplicate those processes that Nature does for us free of charge! These are God-given services of our natural capital that we can't even see. These are natural services that humanity requires to survive.

Natural Capitalism lists the natural ecosystems in this country alone that are now threatened by total destruction:

> California wetlands; tall grass prairies; Hawaiian dry forests; forest wetlands in the South; ancient ponderosa pine forests; Southern Appalachian spruce-fir forests; Midwestern wetlands and grasslands; ancient redwood forests, ancient cedar forest in the Northwest. Pine forests of the Great Lakes. We must stop the cutting now while we still have trees left!

Peter Raven, biologist and Director of the Missouri

Botanical Garden, is one of the world's top experts in biodiversity – which he defines as "the functioning of a healthy Earth." He says that putting a cash value on our natural capital…

> says nothing about our real place in nature, morality, or the simple joy of living in a richly diverse, interesting, living world. As a biologist, I always think about such broad subjects in the way the world functions, as if there were no people there…the flow of energy from the sun, and the activities of all the photosynthetic organisms, the food chains and communities that regulate the flow of the stored energy here on Earth, and the ways in which human beings impact or break that flow, or divert it for their own purposes – what are the actual biological limits? For me, it is always the centrality of those functions, within which we evolved and which are so essential to our continued existence, that keeps looming so large.

Herman Daly, photo courtesy of The Wege Foundation

My friend Herman Daly, former World Bank economist, says humanity stands at a pivotal crossroads. For the first time in history, our economy's increase in prosperity is limited not by a lack of human-made capital, but by the lack of natural capital. We can build spaceships and nuclear power plants. But we can NOT manufacture trees and water and soil and biological diversity.

We must begin to establish values for our finite natural capital, as rough as those estimates might be. At the same time, we must behave as if there were a cost involved when we use up Earth's natural resources. Setting a price on them is a first step toward incorporating the value of ecosystem services into planning, policy, and public behavior. We have no time to waste.

If we as a civilization

Had wisdom, understanding, and knowledge,

We would not have war, overpopulation, and environmental destruction.

Humanity's goal must be Peace.

The way to Peace is through Education that makes us wise.

Wisdom teaches us to balance Nature, our Natural Capital,

With the Economy, our financial capital.

That is Economicology.

Peter M. Wege, 2008

CHAPTER 14

SELF-RENEWAL: The Individual and the Innovative Society

...the source of creativity for the society is in the person. Renewal springs from the freshness and vitality of individual men and women.

John W. Gardner

In 1963, John Gardner, my friend and environmental hero, wrote a small book titled *Self-Renewal* with the subtitle *The Individual and The Innovative Society*. In 1981, he published an updated version of *Self-Renewal*. I cherish my copy of the revised book as John wrote this inside the cover: "To Peter Wege, with admiration and good wishes from his friend." It's signed in John's familiar scroll with a big, loopy "J."

In this revised book, Gardner wrote that of the many factors involved in "self-renewal," he thought motivation was the most important. And despite the good things that had failed to happen since his first book had been published almost twenty years earlier, Gardner remained hopeful. In fact, he used the term "tough-minded optimism" as he called all Americans to continue the good environmental fight.

In addition to advocating a positive attitude about saving the environment, he also called for "staying power." Since life is an ongoing struggle, Gardner wrote we must have "a hard-bitten morale" so that we can "strive with every ounce of our energy to prevail." He knew the task of renewing ourselves as a nation and as individuals would be hard. But he had faith we could do it.

Since my friend John first published this book in 1963, many things have happened to shake our "tough-minded optimism." For me, the future does not seem as certain as it was when I received my Army Air Force wings in May of 1943. My seven children are now almost twice as old as I was when I earned my pilot's wings. Yet over those years, the world has not progressed as fast as John Gardner and I had hoped.

But his call for a tough kind of optimism and strong moral fiber help keep me moving forward. If we listen to John Gardner's plea for self-renewal, we will start using our intelligence, education, and moral strength. We will work together to end wars and renew the world with common sense.

If we had a better understanding of what civilization really means, we could start negotiating with the world's leading nations toward the common goal of World Peace. Millions of people are praying for the leaders of the world to make this happen. But John Gardner made it clear that these prayers must also include honest and fair criticisms at the same time.

In *Self-Renewal,* Gardner wrote:

> A tradition of vigorous criticism is essential to the renewal of a society. A nation is not helped much by citizens whose love for their country leads them to shield it from life-giving criticism… neither uncritical lovers nor unloving critics make for the renewal of societies.

When our leaders in Washington refuse to enforce environmental laws already on the books, we have a patriotic and moral obligation to criticize those elected public servants. Yet, at the same time we call them to account for their failure to act, we must also be civilized in the way we do it. But if we are to truly renew ourselves and our society, Gardner made it clear that we must challenge those leaders who are not doing their jobs.

Gardner wrote:

> Finally, we shall renew neither ourselves, nor our society, nor a troubled world unless we share a vision of something worth saving.... We have the difficult task of facing the threat (of nuclear war) and at the same time looking beyond it. If we fail to look beyond it...we shall forget what kind of world we might have wished to build had we been granted peace.

If we are to be "granted peace," governments must act now to end the illiterate terrorism that is tearing our world apart. We must come together under the United Nations with all the major countries supporting this goal. The time is now. We have enough intelligent leaders in place. Together they must face up to the rogue nations if we're ever to have a lasting peace.

Father Theodore M. Hesburgh, C.S.C., president emeritus of the University of Notre Dame, is a friend who once shared a good idea with me. He suggested that under the United Nations' leadership, we create an International Military so powerful that the rogue nations couldn't stand up to them. With the best Army, Navy, and Air Force in the world, all under intelligent and civilized leadership, the illiterate terrorists could no longer drag the free world into war. War MUST be eliminated if we are to save the world from annihilation. And each of us can help make that happen. My friend John Gardner had great faith in the individual American citizen's ability to change the world in ways as profound as ending warfare.

Gardner wrote that the "source of creativity for the society is in the person. Renewal springs from the freshness and vitality of individual men and women." As individual leaders and as nations, we must drop our egos and grab our ecos. This means ending wars. It also means promoting economicology.

In March 2007, Johnnie L. Roberts published an editorial in *Newsweek Magazine* with a headline that supports economicology: *The Street Turns Green.* In his article, Roberts explains how the brokerage firm Goldman Sachs, now emerging from its financial problems, had to collaborate with environmentalists in order to buy TXU, a polluting Texas utility. This was a huge deal that Goldman badly wanted to broker.

The result of the economists and ecologists working together is that TXU had to cut the number of new coal-fired plants they'd planned to build from 11 to three. In addition to slashing eight new polluting plants, Goldman and its investors committed to spending four hundred million dollars on energy-saving research such as wind power.

The editorial says:

> Wall Street is experiencing a climate change. Elite global investment banks like Citi, J.P. Morgan and Merrill Lynch never used to think twice about filling up the tanks of the nation's biggest polluters looking for cash. But now, many of the same banks that grew rich financing companies' strip mines, oil rigs, and SUV plants are advising clients that the way to get the green is to go green.

While it's taken the financial community a long time to recognize the principle of economicology, I'm gratified to see that they are finally getting it. What's good for our ecology is good for economy. What harms our ecology harms our economy.

In the same editorial, Mindy Lubber, president of a network of investors, environmentalists, and public advocates, summarized economicology. She described investment banks like Goldman Sachs as "very welcome players in what is as much an economic as a science and environmental discussion."

> Thou shalt not commit abuse against the Earth
> and its life-support system, but rather honor it
> with respect for sustaining life.
>
> Peter M. Wege
> *ECONOMICOLOGY: The Eleventh Commandment*

CHAPTER 15

Lindsey Grant on the Crisis of Overpopulation

We finally have to figure how many people we can
support based on our ability to provide a healthy
and viable living experience.

Peter M. Wege
Grand Rapids Press Editorial Letter

In reviewing Lindsey Grant's book *Too Many People*
published in 2000, I find that his title and arguments
are what most of the civilized world is hoping for. We
simply have "too many people" for our planet. Lindsey
Grant clearly states that family planning is not just
something we are free to practice or not.

Rather, Grant writes, it is something the Earth
itself must have if we are to escape the damage of
continued human population growth. According to
Lindsey Grant, family planning is "essential to the
preservation of ecological balance in the face of a
species grown far too successful."

But Lindsey Grant's call for controlling the growth of
the world's population is not attainable without raising
the level of education. Many people reading Grant's
book might say it is "pie in the sky" or wishful thinking.
But most of us truly believe curtailing the birth rate is
possible, even if it takes decades to achieve.

As I read through *Too Many People,* I thought back
on the history of this world and how strong leadership
is always called for in a time of crisis. Producing more
people than the world's natural resources can support

is just such a time of crisis. Today we need powerful leaders who will adopt Grant's workable, deadly serious plan. I wholeheartedly agree with Grant when he says that if we neglect to take this problem seriously now, we can count on an unlivable planet within the next hundred years.

Grant writes:

> Our future depends on learning to come into better balance with the rest of nature and to find a sustainable relationship we have yet to achieve… (I) make the case that we can turn the present deteriorating system around only by ending the worldwide infatuation with growth and embracing the idea of a return to a smaller population

We know, as Grant repeatedly states, we can't grow infinitely on the finite space of one planet. And the only way to solve our out-of-control census numbers is to implement a negative population growth (NPG). It is the one solution that can turn back the runaway numbers of new births we continue to record. NPG is the only way we can attain what Grant calls a "less destructive and more tolerable level" of global population.

But we have no hope of reaching NPG without the help of the world's major religions. Lindsey Grant's book can accomplish nothing unless we enlist religious leaders from around the globe to help control human-population growth. We need to hold a world conference of the major religions so that all faiths can come together to teach their congregations the need for stewardship of the planet that is home to us all. That stewardship begins with controlling the number of people who live on it

Religions must stop competing with each other and instead seek a common ground to work out their different views on family planning. The world's major religions must find a way to consolidate their intelligence and help control the world's population for all the right reasons.

Over thirty years ago in his 1977 book *Steady State Economics,* my friend Herman Daly was already warning the world that our passion for unrestricted growth would ultimately destroy the human race. Steady-state economics, according to Daly, requires a constant supply of physical wealth – or capital – matched by a constant stock of people. Now into the 21st Century, we are sadly proving how prophetic Daly was. Our world now faces the disaster of overpopulation AND a rising rate of capital consumption.

Lindsey Grant is a humanitarian who reminds us that it is the world's poorest people who most need the benefits of family planning. Where once primitive conditions limited family size through an absence of medicine, sanitation, and sufficient food, society has improved those natural causes of death. What this means, Grant writes, is that "family planning is perhaps the most fundamental advance in the human condition."

By limiting the size of our families by choice, we are no longer "waiting for the control to come from misery and rising mortality."

In other words, by controlling the growth of our human species through regulating fertility, we prevent endless human suffering. By limiting the size of our families by choice, we are no longer "waiting for the control to come from misery and rising mortality." Parents living in the Third World countries will gain the most because their children will no longer be "trapped in high mortality."

The principles of economicology I have advocated all my life can never be fulfilled until we solve this vital problem presented in Grant's book *Too Many People.*

As he writes:

> Defining an optimum population and learning how
> to reach it with family planning are central to any
> hope of an environmentally sustainable future.

In offering some "goal" numbers of people this
planet can sustain, Lindsey Grant first spells out
why we are in a population crisis. In 1900, the U.N.
estimated the Earth supported 1.6 billion people. That
number has ballooned to over 6.8 billion today with
7.5 billion projected for 2020 – not that far away.

As Grant makes clear, it is the less developed
countries (LDC) with high disease and low wages
that are reproducing themselves the fastest despite
the ravages of AIDS and starvation. Population in the
LDC jumps by some 75 million people a year! Over
the next half century, this LDC census is expected to
climb another 73 percent and comprise 87 percent of
the world's population by 2050.

Considering that our finite planet is supporting well
over six billion people now, consider what Lindsey
Grant projects as ideal numbers. This author, who is
an expert on what resources the human population
requires, writes that a satisfactory global GNP can
support "perhaps one billion" people.

Grant also addresses what has finally become a
mainstream conversation around water coolers and
in Washington: the long-term impact of global climate
change. If we are to have any chance of avoiding
the disasters of man-made climate warming, Grant
projects the world's population could be no higher than
three billion – less than half of where we are today.

Grant writes:

> We are already at war with the biosphere that
> supports us. More than any other proposed

solution, a solution on the demand side – population – offers an effective way to end or ameliorate the problems I have described. It works across all those sectors, and, remarkably enough, it will save money rather than demanding more investments.

The last sentence in this passage brings us right back to the principles of economicology. By doing the right thing for our ecology – controlling human population – we will always be helping the economy. The most expensive things we are doing now is trying to fix the environmental destruction we humans have caused. By having more people than our finite planet can support, we have polluted the air, contaminated land, and dirtied and diminished our fresh water. Cleaning up the air, soil, and water is a huge cost that will burden our children and grandchildren for generations to come. That is assuming we can even fix the ecological destruction we have done.

Instead of passing that burden on, we need to start living by the code of my Six Es. The attitude of the Six Es toward the Earth will give future generations the healthy planet they deserve to inherit. Our Ecology is sacred and finite. This Environment is the only home we'll ever have. Our Economy cannot survive on an Earth lacking healthy air, water, and land because too many people need it.

Education is our best hope for controlling population growth. We will do this out of our Empathy for each other, especially the most vulnerable in the less developed nations. Finally, we must support family planning around the globe because it is the moral thing to do, and it is our Ethics that makes us human and advances civilization.

. The Preamble to the Earth Charter repeats what Lindsey Grant has written in *Too Many People* and what I have talked about for over thirty years:

An unprecedented rise in human population has overburdened ecological and social systems. The foundations of global security are threatened. These trends are perilous – but not inevitable.

I always look for the positive, not the negative. To me, the glass is always half full, not half empty. So while I share Lindsey Grant's view that the population increases are "perilous," I also believe they are not "inevitable." Through education, through raising the level of intelligence, we can limit population growth to what the planet can sustain. The short poem I wrote here summarizes my faith that we can save the planet, and educating people around the globe is the key.

Time waits for no one; man and woman too;
Now's the time to move, the future's up to you.
We have to pass on what we know
To make our positive energy grow.
Together we can make a go
With EDUCATION: let it flow!

Peter M. Wege

CHAPTER 16

PLAN B 2.0: Rescuing a Planet Under Stress and a Civilization in Trouble

The days of the fossil fuel-based, automobile-centered, throwaway economy are numbered.

Lester R. Brown

Lester Brown called his first book in 2003 *PLAN B.* He chose that title because he'd concluded that Earth's plan A of doing business as usual was not working. A plan B, as we all know, is a fall-back position when our first plan, A, has failed. The response to Brown's first book *PLAN B* was so overwhelming that the author, president of Earth Policy Institute in Washington D.C., realized he had to write a follow-up book. *PLAN B 2.0* is the updated and expanded version of his earlier book.

Some of his chapter topics point to why plan A failed and why a new plan B is necessary for the planet's survival. One of the most pressing topics – that the world has finally recognized – is what Brown titles a chapter in *PLAN B 2.0,* "The Coming Decline of Oil."

Scientists, geologists, and now even money-blinded oil companies recognize that most of the world's oil has already been discovered. As geologist Colin Campbell put it, "The whole world has now been systemically searched and picked over...it is almost inconceivable now that major fields remain to be found."

Long overdue, but at last the world's major oil companies have accepted the fact that our planet's supply of fossil fuels is finite, not infinite. This belated awareness has caused them to focus on the reserves they already have which will only add to the cost of gasoline. Without new oil coming online, and with OPEC controlling how much oil gets to the market, it is just a matter of time until gas goes right back up to four dollars-plus a gallon. One hundred dollar barrels will look cheap to us!

But it's not just how much drivers will have to pay filling up their inefficient, gas-guzzling SUVs. It's about feeding the poor. Today's farmers also rely on gas and diesel to plant and harvest their crops. Manufacturing fertilizers takes a lot of energy. Yet with the rising cost of oil over the last half century, farmers will have an increasingly harder time making enough money selling their crops to pay for their energy needs.

There is another factor, however, to consider. We are running short of arable land. For the farmer, the silver lining is that the shortage of good soil will raise the price of food. And farmers need to sell their food for enough money so they can make a living. American farmers and their farms are a precious resource.

Look what's happened to farmers' incomes since the oil crunch began. Back in 1950, farmers could sell a bushel of their wheat for $1.89 and buy a barrel of oil for $1.71 – a 1:1 ratio. By 2005, the price for that bushel of wheat had doubled to $3.90, but the cost of the oil to produce it had gone up to $52 – a 1:13 ratio!

When OPEC began pushing up the price of oil in the early 1970s, it created the greatest transfer of wealth in history to countries whose leaders are not all our friends. Suddenly Saudi Arabia, Kuwait, Iraq, and Iran were awash in money that drastically increased energy costs for farmers who feed the world.

But instead of despairing over what our dependence on fossil fuel has done to our ecology and to our economy, I share Brown's view that we have the solutions. We only need the will to use them. The hybrid cars I've been buying since Honda brought the first ones to this country offer one solution. Now my staff and I drive hybrids made by Ford and Toyota as well. Hybrid cars and trucks are not a passing fancy. They are the first round of the alternative-energy car engines that will replace the gas-guzzling combustion motors. Hydrogen-powered fuel cells will power the next generation of automobiles. Lester Brown predicts the 88,000 hybrids sold in this country in 2004 will be an historic low. In 2007, Americans bought 350,000 hybrids, so Brown's on track with his forecast.

The next step has to be developing cars that run on hydrogen, which means their residue is H_2O – water! We are at least a decade away from seeing hydrogen cars on the road in any quantities. The refueling stations needed to fill the cars with hydrogen will have to be developed creating a new and cleaner infrastructure. A whole new industry will grow out of building those hydrogen stations.

Earth is losing lakes and water sources at a frightening pace.

But an even more serious threat than diminishing fossil fuel supplies looms for our world, according to Lester Brown. Earth is losing lakes and water sources at a frightening pace. Not enough oil will continue to create great economic, environmental, and social turmoil – including tragedies like the war in Iraq. But since we don't drink oil, we can live without it. Water, on the other hand, is a necessity for all living things.

One of the many environmental disasters created under the totalitarian rule of the Soviet Union was diverting the two rivers feeding the Aral Sea in order to create cotton fields for manufacturing textiles. The Aral Sea fishing industry that once produced 50,000 tons a year has disappeared, as have the thousands of jobs related to catching and processing fish.

In China, over 20,000 lakes have disappeared in the last 20 years. Mexico's expanding population is outgrowing that country's water supply. Lake Chapala, Mexico's largest, is the primary source of water for the five million people who live in Guadalajara. Expanded irrigation for crops has reduced Lake Chapala's volume by 80 percent.

The people of Pakistan depend on the Indus River for their water. However, Pakistan's massive population expansion – expected to reach 305 million by 2050 – is already taking more water than the Indus can spare. This life-giving river supplying water for the growing number of people in this Muslim nation is already running dry in its lowest reaches.

But we aren't doing much better in this country. The 200-square-mile Owens Lake in California has disappeared since its precious water supply was diverted to Los Angeles in 1913. Mono Lake, the oldest lake in North America and a major food station for migrating birds, has dropped 35 feet since 1941 when that California lake was also diverted to Los Angeles.

But, again, we must be optimistic. We have provable ways to stabilize our water supply. In Australia, closing down the Mowamba aqueduct after a century of altering nature's river patterns has already raised the level and flow of the Snowy River. The Snowy River is expected to regain 28 percent of its natural level which will restore its natural functions. In this country we have demolished hundreds of small dams that will help restore river flows and reinvigorate the fishing industry.

Another successful effort to return rivers to their natural health has been going on in California since 1992. Environmental efforts to increase the flow of the Sacramento-San Joaquin Rivers – which merge before emptying into San Francisco Bay – helped protect the Bay's rich aquatic system. Over 120 species of fish depend on this particular ecosystem for their survival.

In PLAN B 2.0, Lester Brown also addresses the

Photo taken by Peter M. Wege

disastrous ways humans have treated our planet's once rich and lush forests. In 1900, Earth's forested area stood at five billion hectares. Today, we are down to 3.9 billion hectares. But we never seem to learn the significance of those frightening numbers until the consequences of our short-sightedness cause human tragedy.

Not until flash floods and landslides caused by massive deforestation killed 340 people in the Philippines in 2004 did the government act. Suddenly the police and military were ordered to go after illegal loggers. Similarly Thailand banned tree cutting only after floods and landslides killed a large number of their citizens. And not until China experienced $30 billion in damage from the Yangtze flooding did that government outlaw all tree cutting in the Yangtze basin that is home to 400 million people.

But again Lester Brown's *PLAN B 2.0* shares my view that all is not lost. Solutions are as simple as reducing the amount of wood we use to make paper in the developing world – with all our advanced non-paper communications like email and text messaging, that can easily be done – and developing countries will need to reduce the amount of wood they use for fuel.

The good news is that we are making progress. As the world's largest consumer of paper, the United States has the chance to become the world's biggest tree savers. Twenty years ago, maybe one-fourth of the paper we used in the USA was recycled. But by 2003, that figure had risen to 48 percent. We *can* do it when we get educated about the need to do so.

Similarly, in the undeveloped world, alternative fuels are already being developed. In Kenya, for instance, inexpensive solar cookers made from cardboard and aluminum foil use sunshine to cook a complete meal. These solar cookers pasteurize the water which saves lives. Electric hotplates fed by wind-generated electricity will also diminish the demand on wood for fuel.

I've been pounding the table for so long about our need to save paper in order to protect the planet's trees that I made up a simple poem. Some day I would like to see it written on every paper towel dispenser in every public bathroom in this country:

Why take two? One will do!

Peter M. Wege

Michigan Autumn, photo taken by Peter M. Wege

CHAPTER 17

Confronting Consumption

We are living in a material world, and I am
a material girl.

Madonna

Madonna's hit song pretty well speaks for the
value Americans place on accumulating and using
up "things." We should be embarrassed by the fact
that while Americans make up only one percent of
the world's population, we consume 25 percent of
the world's goods. In 2009, a popular movie titled
Shopaholic came out spoofing American's addiction to
shopping. The film was classified as a comedy despite
the destructive truth of over-consumption that was
being satirized.

But fortunately for the environment, some smart
university environmentalists have taken on the
sensitive issue of America's excessive consumerism.
Three college professors collaborated on the book
named for its message and advocacy: *Confronting
Consumption*. Thomas Princen, University of
Michigan, Michael Maniates, Allegheny College,
and Ken Conca, University of Maryland, assert that
a major focus of environmental thinking and action
must start dealing with the issue of consumerism.
Now known for our "conspicuous consumption,"
Americans need to lead the charge by changing
our ways if the planet is to survive.

Around the globe, mankind's currently extravagant

and wasteful habits must change, as this book makes clear. These three academicians use solid research to prove their case on the need for Americans to alter our daily usage patterns. The book also offers us hope by writing about some visionary thinkers who are already taking actions to reduce "the accumulation frenzy" this country seems to be on.

The word I coined in 1998, economicology, summarizes my philosophy. If we are to save our miraculously diverse planet, we must seek a balance between our ecology and our economy. Without a healthy environment, there can be no healthy economy. These three college professors have confirmed my faith in this principle by linking environmental and economic needs.

Consider the distressing fact that one third of the United States' municipal solid waste is made up of discarded packaging!

Americans create more waste than any other nation in the world. In 1960, Americans were creating an average of 2.7 pounds of waste a day. By 1998, not even 40 years later, we were up to an average of 4.5 pounds of waste a day for each person! This growing consumerism endangers our ecology because we have also increased the production of synthetic materials that don't degrade naturally.

The use of extravagant packaging, especially non-degradeable plastics, has combined to make waste disposal a major environmental hazard. Consider the distressing fact that one third of the United States' municipal solid waste is made up of discarded packaging! Consider the fact that 87 percent of the one billion plastic water bottles Americans bought in 2007 ended up in landfills and waterways.

This expansion of plastics in our landfills would not have happened had we not become a throw-away, consumer-mad society. The proliferation of malls and shopping centers, mail catalogues, and now Internet sales have swamped us in material goods we can buy.

The authors write:

> ...consumers are purchasing more and more 'stuff' and throwing more of it away when its relatively short, useful life is over. The quantity and availability of 'stuff' that makes this culture of consumption possible, however, are also intimately linked to the mass-production and consumption systems facilitated by economic globalization...as incomes rise, material consumption and its corresponding wastes also tend to increase.

Advancing technology, like bigger and faster computers, exacerbate the waste problem. When a personal computer becomes obsolete after a few years, getting rid of it creates an entirely new threat to our environment. And since buying a new PC has become cheaper than updating an old one, that's exactly what we do. In 1998 alone, 20 million PCs were discarded with only 10 percent recycled to churches and schools. That means most computers end up in landfills bringing with them their levels of heavy metals including lead and cadmium.

If we're ever going to change these throw-away habits, we must educate all people on the necessity of preserving a livable environment based on ethics and respect for the natural system. We need to act now! What is happening to these dangerous waste materials – like lead-acid batteries – is that we are actually shipping them to poorer nations in Latin America and Asia where there are far fewer environmental restrictions. Americans and Europeans who carefully rinse out their plastic containers for recycling have no idea that most of them will end up in Indonesia where they are not recycled but dumped in landfills.

In a 2007 Grand Rapids, Michigan, meeting of mayors from Great Lakes cities and two Canadian provinces, Dick Miller, Mayor of Toronto, addressed the controversial issue of his city's exporting their trash to our state. Toronto began paying to ship its municipal waste to Michigan after Canadian residents fought a new landfill in an abandoned mine 600 kilometers north of the city. The people living in the community where the proposed landfill was to go raised such a ruckus that Michigan became the "political" solution.

But we Michigan residents have not ever been happy with that solution to Toronto's waste problem. As the keynote speaker for the Great Lakes Mayors meeting, Mayor Miller assured his Grand Rapids audience that Toronto was not going to ship any more trash to Michigan after 2008. The audience broke into spirited applause.

I have always tried to focus on solutions to environmental damage rather than the problems themselves. In *Confronting Consumption,* the three professors do just that. The third part of the book is devoted to suggestions and ideas about ways every caring American can help slow down our over-the-top consumerism. The most significant change, because it can affect all our purchasing decisions, is developing a new mind set that says less is, indeed, more. We must wake up to the reality that having more "things" never has and never can make us better or happier people.

Some call this new awareness "simple living" or "voluntary simplicity." It's also referred to as "downsizing." How often have you heard someone say, "I need to simplify my life." That's the attitude we must all acquire if we are to curtail our runaway consumerism. More and more of us are doing just that. In fact, people who actually do simplify their lives by downsizing tell their friends they now rush less, work less, want less, and spend less. Their own conclusion is that they're far happier than they were in their previous high-accumulation days.

As the authors write, "Simple living in an age of instant gratification and globalized mass consumption deserves our attention."

A second positive way to fight excessive consumerism is supporting a small but growing grassroots movement that's taking aim at the intoxicating world of advertising. Based in Canada, these intelligent and visionary writers, graphic artists, and volunteers have collaborated to create the Adbusters Media Foundation. One of the several ways they educate the public about the deceptive world of advertising is through their award-winning magazine, *Adbusters: Journal of the Mental Environment.*

For example, they share the ugly American statistics on how greedy we are for things. One article states:

> The average North American consumes five times more than a Mexican, ten times more than a Chinese person, and thirty times more than a person from India.... Give it a rest, America. Tomorrow is Buy Nothing Day.

Indeed, Buy Nothing Day is one of Adbusters' annual holidays to raise Americans' consciousness about the destructive power of over consuming. TV Turn-Off Week and World Car-Free Day are two other international events sponsored and promoted by Adbusters.

And they are out to expose the phoniness of Big Advertising by fighting them on their own terms: with high-profile, glossy, polished ads. Only Adbusters uses the slick advertising approach to mock the deceptiveness of big corporate ad spenders.

With advertising bombarding us on everything from football helmets to golf bags, from buses to bathrooms, not to mention TV, radio and the Internet, Americans encounter some 3,000 ads every day. By the age of 18, every American has been exposed to 360,000 ads. Annual spending on advertising in the U.S. alone has gone from $6.5 billion in 1950 to $170 billion in 2006!

The competition among advertisers for the consumer's attention has led to an increase in ads using sex, violence, and pure shock. Talk about brainwashing, how about the small children pushing toy shopping carts around Wal-Mart stores that read, "Wal-Mart Shopper in Training?" The title of the Adbusters magazine is right on target by calling itself *The Journal of the Mental Environment*.

It is the mental environment we need to address. When consumers go shopping in response to an ad, it's almost an addictive reaction. They think they "have" to have it because they saw it advertised on television.

Kalle Lasn, cofounder and editor of Adbusters writes that we have been kidnapped by the billion-dollar-a-year advertising industry and the corporations behind it who are giving us this dream of never-ending material progress. They're conditioning us to a false reality.

I have long supported the holistic approach to health that integrates the human mind, the body, and the spirit as one entity. That's actually the name of a hospital wing I helped build in my dad's memory: The Wege Institute of Mind, Body, and Spirit. The Institute treats illness by addressing all three. Adbusters' editor Kalle Lasn endorses this need to balance the mind and the body and the spirit when she writes:

> Mental disease has become the number two
> health problem in the world...people (need to)
> start making the connections between advertising
> and their own mental health...

I agree with Lasn and this book's three authors that we need to take a far more serious look at advertising. We need to pay attention to the destructive effects it has on our consumerism which, in turn, directly

Image courtesy of adbusters.org

damages the environment. I heartily commend Adbusters for its emphasis on educating the public about both our extravagant buying and about the almost hypnotic effects of advertising.

I have long maintained that the educational system in our country is outmoded. Education is our key to the future, and we must teach our young people – especially teenagers – how their excessive buying of things is jeopardizing the future of their planet. They need to learn about the fragility of our natural system and understand that protecting it is the key to our survival as a civilization.

For many years, I have said and written that we must educate people about the mind, body, and spirit connection. We must educate them about economicology. I applaud the three authors of *Confronting Consumption* for what they are contributing to this goal. I close this chapter with a quotation from the book capturing the attitude of American shoppers that makes us consume one-fourth of all the world's goods while we are only one percent of the Earth's people.

> Goods are good and more goods are better.... Production reigns supreme because consumption is beyond scrutiny.

> *Confronting Consumption*

CHAPTER 18

The Great Lakes Water Wars

by Peter Annin

The year 2009 supplied more good news on saving our Great Lakes than any other in my lifetime! And whoever pegged the 20th as the Century of Oil and the 21st as the Century of Water was absolutely right. Living things can survive without a lot of other things – including oil – but water is not one of them.

Peter Annin, a former Newsweek columnist, wrote a book in 2006 titled *The Great Lakes Water Wars*. Annin's book just might turn out to be one of the most important warnings ever written on the threatened natural resource of the Great Lakes considering what has happened since its publication. With the five Lakes containing 95 percent of this country's fresh surface water and 18 percent of the Earth's, Annin said in 2006 that the Lakes were on the radar screen of parched nations.

According to Annin, over the next century the world will become increasingly divided between the water "haves" and the water "have-nots," with most have-nots among the poorest nations. That means tensions will increase "as water scarcity becomes a divisive political issue throughout the world." People living in dry areas "will demand that water-rich regions 'share' their resource with the rest of the world."

Annin says Peter Gleick, a global water expert, does not like the term 'water wars.' But still Gleick acknowledges that "…water is increasingly a factor in conflict, and there's a long history of violence over water, and I think it's going to get worse."

Gleick has researched wars over water back to 3000 B.C and continuing to the present. In 1935, for instance, the Arizona National Guard was mobilized in a dispute with California over water in the Colorado River. Asia, with 60 percent of the world's population but only 36 percent of the Earth's water, could well become a combatant if the world were ever to actually fight over the Great Lakes water.

Facing the reality of the disparity in fresh water around the globe, the dreaded "d" word, diversion, has become an increasing topic of public debate. The idea of diverting Great Lakes water is not new. Both the Canadians and Americans in the Great Lakes Basin have feared this for decades, even from thirsty citizens within their own countries. Our own southwest desert greatly needs more water.

But because of the cost to ship fresh water from the Great Lakes to California, for instance, some government officials don't worry about it. Even the 2000 report of the International Joint Commission created in 1909 to resolve water disputes between the U.S. and Canada downplayed the risk of major water diversion and transfers. But both Annin and I agree that was a risky assumption.

Lake Michigan, the Great Lake closest to my hometown of Grand Rapids, is particularly tempting to parched lands around the globe. It is the second largest of the five by volume and third in surface area. That's why Michigan's leaders were encouraged by a collaborative report issued in 2005.

That year the eight Great Lakes Governors and two premiers of Ontario and Quebec published their findings after six years of studying water issues. The finished versions of the long awaited documents were called the Great Lakes-St. Lawrence River Basin Sustainable Water Resources Agreement and its companion Compact. While the Agreement is voluntary, the Compact is designed to become a set of legally binding regulations.

But before either the Agreement or the Compact could go into effect, all eight states and the United States Congress had to agree on the regulations that affect the United States' side of the Canadian border. In order to protect this planet's most abundant freshwater reservoir, our two national governments, all eight Great Lakes states, and two Canadian provinces needed to act as one. This was not a political issue, but an environmental one.

Peter Annin's book cited the ecological catastrophe of the Aral Sea as what could happen if we ever diverted Great Lakes Water. The Aral was once the fourth largest inland body of water in the world. But in the 1950s, Soviet engineers redirected much of the river feeding the Aral to irrigate massive fields. Since then, the water levels in the Aral Sea have fallen 80 feet, and 90 percent of its volume is gone.

Annin writes:

> ...it's tempting to think that the (Great Lakes) Basin's resources are inexhaustible. But if nothing else, the Aral Sea's desiccation shows that large bodies of water like the Great Lakes are not indomitable...the Aral's experience shows that humans do have the power and the ability to destroy natural wonders like the Great Lakes.

Annin's next warning reinforces my theory of economicology:

> ...irreparable harm would come to the regional ecosystem and economy.... Large lakes have limits. If care is not taken in their management, ecological and economic disaster will follow. In other words, if we destroy the ecology of the Great Lakes, we will destroy the economy for the 40 million people who live and work there.

In 1985-86, a severe drought in New York City caused officials there to look toward the Great Lakes for water, focusing on Lake Ontario or Lake Erie. "It's inescapable," New York's environmental commissioner Henry Williams said at the time, "that the abundant water supply in the Great Lakes will be included in any consideration of water allocation in New York State."

But since at the time Governor Mario Cuomo had just signed the voluntary Great Lakes Charter to preserve the Lakes' water, he could not very well suddenly campaign to divert water from one of those Lakes! While it never happened, the threat was real.

As Annin writes:

> The scare from New York only reinforced the Charter's non-binding nature, and some Great Lakes leaders hungered for something more... these officials believed that a legally binding statute was still necessary to throw down a barrier against large-scale Great Lakes diversions.... They set their eyes on amending the federal Water Resources Development Act (WRDA)...federal legislation that is renewed periodically for major public-works projects.

The first section of Annin's book ended with some "Hope and Hopelessness":

> The governors and premiers had gone from having no regimen for regulating Great Lakes diversions to having two very different and somewhat awkward water-management systems.... One was voluntary, but international. The other was binding, but domestic – and of questionable constitutionality...

Unfortunately, so much time, energy, and political capital had been spent drawing up these two ineffective agreements that, Annin explains, by the later 1980s there was little energy to do anything more.

Regional officials would have to live with what had been adopted and hope it provided some protection.

This whole idea of diverting Great Lakes water to supply dry areas beyond our basin would violate all my Six E principles. Education, as in the Aral Sea example, shows us how water diversion can come back to haunt us in the environmental damage it causes. Damaging the Ecology and Environment of the Great Lakes will do irreparable harm. The Great Lakes' Economy, second only to that of the federal government's, would suffer.

Maybe most important, it is a contradiction of our Ethics to abuse one of God's greatest wonders in the five Great Lakes. The harm it would do those living in the Great Lakes basin violates the principle of Empathy where we must look at the world from our fellow man's point of view.

CHAPTER 19

The Dreaded 'D' Word

Annin calls Part II in *Water Wars*, "Battle Lines and Skirmishes." One of the early battles over water was reversing the flow of the Chicago River in the late 19th Century. This drastic measure was to improve the public health by shipping the city's raw sewage away from Lake Michigan and dumping it elsewhere. In this case, the recipient of Chicago's offal was the Illinois River! While it was hailed as an engineering feat at the time, it proved to be an environmental disaster.

Redirecting Chicago's sewage first to the Illinois River and from there to the Mississippi did, indeed, clean up Chicago. But it also, according to the former environment commissioner for Chicago, became "the poster child of bad behavior in the Great Lakes."

In 1930, the Supreme Court forced Chicago to start building sewage treatment plants and stop shipping its sewer pollution into other rivers by 1939. But the damage was already done. Annin quotes from a report by Stanley Chagnon, chief of the Illinois State Water Survey who wrote in 1994:

> Few would argue that through the late 1800s, Chicago residents faced serious health problems due to the quality of their drinking water.... Many, however, have argued that Chicago...did not have the right to divert water from Lake Michigan for its own use and then return that water in a contaminated state and to pollute other waters.

But the city of Chicago was not done exploiting Great Lakes water for its own benefit. In 1967, The Supreme Court allowed Chicago's suburbs to tap into the city's Lake Michigan water even when the suburbs were far outside the Great Lakes Basin.

Annin writes:

> That some of Chicago's western suburbs – located far beyond the Great Lakes Basin line – are drinking Lake Michigan water seems patently unfair to contemporary opponents of Great Lakes diversions. And there are a number of water-troubled communities in other Great Lakes states that would love to access Great Lakes water, but because these areas lie outside the Basin line, their water access has been limited.

Then in 1988, Illinois once again tried to divert water. Annin writes:

> A proposal was on the table to divert water from the Great Lakes to aid people who lived hundreds of miles outside the Basin. This was precisely the kind of out-of-Basin diversion precedent that the Great Lakes Charter and the Water Resources Development Act had tried to prevent.

When Illinois Governor Jim Thompson supported this diversion only three years after he'd signed the Great Lakes Charter to stop such diversions, he rightly infuriated his fellow Great Lakes governors.

Annin writes:

> Governor Tony Early of Wisconsin still remembers how angry and incredulous the rest of the Great Lakes governors were. "Very early after the Charter was signed...Jim Thompson came and said, 'Gee you guys, we've got to divert more water so we can float the barges on the Mississippi,'" Governor Early recalls.

To be added, communities beyond Chicago must prove Lake Michigan is the cheapest water source available. If a community withdraws from the deep aquifer, it must stop using groundwater within five years. Cameron Davis of the Alliance for the Great Lakes, and now President Obama's Great Lakes 'tsar,' thinks the other Great Lakes states, especially those on Lake Michigan, should be worried about Illinois' water expansions. "If I were Wisconsin, Indiana, or Michigan, I'd be mad as hell because obviously Illinois is able to play by different rules and continue hooking up communities. Once these communities are hooked up, the ability to unhook them, politically, is pretty much zero."

The hopeful news on conserving Lake Michigan's water use in Chicago came from my friend and fellow environmentalist Chicago's Mayor Daley when he made a daring decision. In 2003, Mayor Daley risked enormous political outrage from his constituents in Chicago by doing the right thing for the Great Lakes. The Windy City residents had always paid one simple fee for all the water they wanted. Daley rewrote that rule making Chicago residents do what all their customer communities were doing: pay for the water they used.

> ...Chicago's era of flat-rate water use was coming to an end. Residents of roughly 320,000 houses and small apartment buildings were told.... For the first time, all Chicagoans would be expected to pay for water on an as-used basis.

Mayor Daley's willingness to always do the right thing for the Great Lakes has endeared him to me and all the HOW-GL leadership. In fact our HOW-GL Coalition held its third annual meeting in Mayor Daley's city in September 2007. Over 300 people from over 100 environmental organizations met at the Palmer House to update our strategy for getting the federal government to pass the $20 billion Great Lakes Collaboration Implementation Act (GLCIA).

Obviously that strategy worked when President Obama signed the $20 billion GLCIA into law on October 30, 2009! Now that this vitally important law is on the books, I'd like to share what I wrote during that meeting on stationery engraved: **The Palmer House Hilton:**

> Dear Concerned Citizens of the Great Lakes Basin:
>
> We are at the right time to change the future of the Great Lakes from degradation to elevation. The Healing Our Waters-Great Lakes Coalition has assembled concerned citizens who belong to the nation's largest environmental organizations. Together these grass-roots Americans number in the millions, and they are actively collaborating to save the Lakes that hold 95 percent of the country's surface fresh water.
>
> United, we must now convince the federal government that this is the time to create lasting legislation that will protect these Great Lakes quality and quantity for the next millennium and beyond... AND WE DID CONVINCE THEM!
>
> ...Together we can do this, and we must do it....
> We must act now to protect these life-giving Lakes.
>
> Peter M. Wege

But the successful signing of the Great Lakes HOW funding is not the end of the story or this chapter. Peter Annin was right to warn us about water wars and the threat of diversions. On December 8, 2008, two years after his book was published, a new Great Lakes-St.Lawrence River Basin Water Resources Compact became effective. This federally approved historic agreement passed by all eight Great Lakes states creates a legal framework to manage water in the Great Lakes basin. According to the Council on State Government, an interstate compact like this is the most powerful, long-lasting, and adaptable mechanism to guarantee cooperation among states.

With the federal government's approval, the Great Lakes states have taken charge of their precious natural resource. This means the topic of "diversion" to drier parts elsewhere won't be on the agenda anymore. And let's pray that everyone reads Peter Annin's book so nobody ever goes to war over water.

A healthy economy needs a healthy Great Lakes.

Jeff Skelding, President of the National Wildlife Federation in his speech at the 2007 HOW-GL conference in Chicago

Lake Michigan Sunset, photo taken by Peter M. Wege

CHAPTER 20

David Ehrenfeld's *The Arrogance of Humanism*

David Ehrenfeld, Professor of Biology at Rutgers University, wrote *The Arrogance of Humanism* in 1972 as a warning that man's technological arrogance was putting the natural world at risk. Now in the 21st Century, what he feared then is even more frightening today. Professor Ehrenfeld, also a medical doctor, has devoted his life to educating people about how prideful – and how wrong! – we are to think this Earth was made just for us.

What Ehrenfeld has defined as the "arrogance of humanism" is the prevalent attitude that lets us feel free to use our man-made technologies so that we can alter nature to please ourselves. Because we humans have started to think the planet was made for us, we continue to rearrange the environment for our own benefit. We see improving technology as a way to make the Earth better for us regardless of the damage we are doing to other forms of life in the process.

In his book, Dr. Ehrenfeld quotes the brilliant scientist Dr. Erwin Chargaff, considered a father of gene research. This man who helped unlock the secrets of genetics also recognized the environmental threat posed by man's sense of superiority. Chargaff wrote:

> This world is given to us on loan. We come and we go; and after a time we leave earth and air and water to others who come after us. My generation, or perhaps the one preceding mine, has been the

first to engage, under the leadership of the exact sciences, in a destructive colonial warfare against nature. The future will curse us for it.

Dr. Chargaff's major discoveries in genetic research proved him to be a gifted scientist. And yet during all his years of meticulous laboratory work researching genes, Dr. Chargaff never lost sight of the big picture. As a brilliant researcher, Dr. Chargaff obviously believed in the pursuit of knowledge. But he also understood the risks of what man might do with new scientific discoveries.

Ehrenfeld reinforces Chargaff's worries about how mankind misuses technological advances made by the scientific community. Ehrenfeld's book asserts that our arrogance as humanists has allowed us to manipulate nature out of our selfishness. Mankind is interested in mankind alone. Ehrenfeld writes:

> 1. Most scientific discoveries and technological inventions can be developed in such a way that they are capable of doing great damage to human beings, their cultures, and their environment.
> 2. If a discovery or a technology can be used for evil purposes, it will be so used.

Ehrenfeld cites genetic engineering – inserting the DNA of one form of life into another – as an example of using scientific gains to engage in dangerous practices. Similarly, technical advances in converting the sun's energy to solar power are beneficial to the planet in energy savings. However, Dr. Ehrenfeld notes that we misuse solar power when we use it to pump water into Arizona because solar energy is so much cheaper than electricity. Thus developers are encouraged to pump far more water than they would if they had to pay to pump it with the more expensive power-line electricity.

Ehrenfeld writes that…*the ability to pump water from the ground at low cost will result in falling water tables, newly dry wells and springs, contamination of underground water with agricultural chemicals, and drastic subsidence of the land above the depleted water reserves.*

René Dubos, the great environmental pioneer I wrote about in my first book, shared Dr. Ehrenfeld's concerns about the environmental damage being done through man's increasing control of technology. Dubos understood that this modern form of arrogant humanism sees mankind as the only life form that matters. This humanistic self-centeredness convinces us that using technology to improve our lives must be the ultimate goal.

In his book *Reason Awake*, Dubos wrote this:

> Developing counter technologies to correct the new kinds of damage constantly being created by technological innovations is a policy of despair. If we follow this course we shall increasingly behave like hunted creatures, fleeing from one protective device to another…we shall be concerned chiefly with sheltering ourselves from environmental dangers while sacrificing the values that make life worth living.

In his book on human arrogance, Ehrenfeld uses the example of the Aswan Dam on the Nile River. The Egyptian people built it to provide irrigation water in their desert land. But while the water helps humans, the silt once carried by the Nile is settling in the reservoirs of Lake Nasser behind the dam. This silting of reservoirs is happening around the globe where man is using technology to build more dams without a thought about the disastrous consequences he is creating.

But the Aswan Dam's equally destructive consequence is that the silt now filling the reservoir once provided valuable nutrients to the Egyptian fields during the annual floods. With the soil-nourishing silt now collected behind the dam, Egyptian farmers must replace it with costly fertilizer. If these two man-made destructive consequences aren't bad enough, damming up the Nile is also wiping out aquatic life.

The decreasing amounts of silt and fresh water flowing into the Mediterranean Sea have raised the water's salinity destroying the Egyptian sardine fishery. My theory of "economicology" is a warning system to prevent exactly such commercial disasters from happening. We can't have a profitable economy without a healthy ecology. By blocking the natural flow of the River Nile to bring water to the Egyptian desert, the government destroyed the water ecology sardines need to live. Countless fishermen and their families were put out of work not because of a bad economy, but because of a destroyed ecology!

Another deadly result of man's tinkering with nature is that the increased number and length of Egypt's irrigation canals have led to a population explosion of snails that carry the terrible disease schistosomiasis, a parasitic infection dangerous to humans, especially children. The irony is that in man's greediness to remake nature for his benefit, he has allowed a nasty human predator to flourish!

Dr. Ehrenfeld goes on to cite man's insatiable need for more power to make human life even more pleasurable as the motive behind building more nuclear power plants. But in our quest for more power to make more "things" to entertain ourselves with, what we destroy in making that extra power doesn't seem to slow us arrogant humanists down. Dr. Ehrenfeld writes that the idea of nuclear power plants supplying "clean fusion power" is a myth encompassing "every environmental delusion of which the humanistic attitude is capable." It ignores the threat of radioactivity, explosions, thermal damage to people and, of course, destruction to the environment.

Worst of all is that we all know what the expanded

nuclear fusion will be used for, the author writes. More snowmobiles to destroy more northern vegetation and shatter the once-quiet months of winter.

Ehrenfeld goes on:

> It will be used to make more laser bombs and surface-to-surface missiles…and more electric outdoor billboards, which will help accelerate the destruction of the meaning of language.

As I said in the chapter about E.O. Wilson's book *The Creation,* we need to tell NASA to come back to Earth. The money we have squandered on space exploration could have been used to preserve and protect this Earth that every living thing depends on. Rutgers biology professor Dr. Ehrenfeld said the same thing in the 1970s.

Ehrenfeld writes:

> The grand delusion of our 'space age' is that we can escape the earthly consequences of our arrogance by leaving the mother planet…for distant celestial bodies…that having fouled this world with our inventions, we will somehow do better in other orbits. However, if one sees humanism for what it is, a religion without God, then the idea is not so strange…. Space is nothing more than a watered-down heaven for modern unbelievers.

In one of Ehrenfeld's quotes by George Wald, I hear my own words and belief. In the *CoEvolution Quarterly,* Wald wrote:

> What bothers me most about Space Colonies – even as concepts – is their betrayal of what I believe to be the deepest and most meaningful human values. I do not think one can life a full

human life without living it among animals
and plants.

I, too, cannot imagine living without the miracles
of nature freely given to us. My profound love and
respect for nature and *all* creatures who share this
planet began when I was a little boy. We had a
German gardener named Herman I used to follow
around in the yard while he explained to me what he
was doing. He had what we call a "green thumb" in
growing plants. But what I remember most was the
reverence Herman had for the forces of nature that
allowed him to plant seeds and watch them flourish.
The arrogant humanists Ehrenfeld has written about
don't understand the mystery and the miracle of
this Earth. Only when we recognize the limits of our
abilities as humans will we be able to feel the joy of
creation. Ehrenfeld asks the hardest question of all:

> Will the things that are being lost – the
> wilderness, the plants and animals…leave too
> vast a gap in the continuity of life to be bridged
> even by the human spirit?

The *Arrogance of Humanism* closes with this poignant
statement by Dr. Ehrenfeld:

> Last night I listened to one of my favorite pieces
> of early baroque music. It reminded me, as it
> always does, of the sea pounding relentlessly
> on a dark beach where I have spent many nights
> waiting to watch the giant sea turtles, last of their
> noble race, heave themselves out of the depths.
> To lay their gleaming eggs in the black sand. The
> music saddened me beyond my power to express,
> because I know that it could not have been written
> in my time; there has been too much progress;
> there is not enough peace.
>
> It saddened me because it reminded me of the
> sea, the sea that gave birth to human beings, that

we carry with us yet in our very cells. It saddened me because it reminded me that in my century, nothing is totally free of the taint of our arrogance. We have defiled everything, much of it forever, even the farthest jungles of the Amazon and the air above the mountains, even the everlasting sea which gave us birth.

I share Ehrenfeld's sadness about what we have done to the planet with "too much progress." I end this chapter with a poem I once wrote that expresses the reverence for the sea I share with Dr. Ehrenfeld. We both recognize the miracle of the sea that "gave birth to human beings."

THE SEA
O changeable sea, triumphant,
Every ripple different as a thumb print.
Now dark, now light, now translucent,
Somber, opaque, frothy, jubilant.
The Master made you as you are,
A divider, an adventurer, a friend.
Systematic in your splendor,
Yet cruel, wild, ready to rend.
From God's eternal sea you gushed
To seal off continents and boundaries.
Lush with seaweed in tidal pools,
Steeped with shadows as the evening cools.
The ebb tide fades away from the shore,
Showing wonders of creation in its every pore

By Peter M. Wege

CHAPTER 21

Roy Beck: Re-Charting America's Future

We must have the courage to believe...

Peter M. Wege

As I move toward the conclusion of this second ECONOMICOLOGY book, I return to what I started with in the first chapter. In his book *Red Sky in The Morning*, Dr. James Gustave 'Gus' Speth, Yale University Dean and Professor in Environmental Policy and Sustainable Development, wrote that the most important of eight steps we must take for a sustainable planet is to control the population.

Dr. Speth calls it "A Stable or Smaller World Population." Gus Speth and I fully agree that limiting the number of people in this world is the environment's and humanity's most important goal. Through *Red Sky* and this book you hold, Dr. Speth and I are on a common mission. We are trying to make people understand that the single greatest threat to our planet, and thus the survival of all life including humankind, is overpopulation.

In June 2008, the U.S. Census Bureau issued its latest projection on how many people this finite Earth will have to support in the too-near future. In 2008, there are already 6.8 billion people dependent on the limited natural resources one world can provide. But within four short years, by 2012, the experts predict a population of seven billion human beings will be drawing on those same resources. To put this frightening growth into perspective, in 1950, the world's population was just over a third of that number. By growing from 2.6 billion to seven billion people in 62 years, we have multiplied the threat of environmental disaster for every living thing – not just humans.

...the single greatest threat to our planet, and thus the survival of all life including humankind, is overpopulation.

Looking back in time is even scarier. From the beginning of human life on Earth until 1800, the human population rose to one billion. It took 130 more years, from 1800 to 1930, to double that number to two billion. This most recent U.S. Census analysis indicates we are adding one billion new people every 13 years! While China is the country with the highest population, followed by India, the United States is third with 304 million people.

In his book *Re-Charting America's Future,* business and environmental writer Roy Beck makes it clear that our country's population increases are not coming from lack of family planning. On the contrary. Americans have chosen to raise smaller families. But Beck argues that our federal government's immigration policies, which are opposed by a majority of Americans, have raised our census numbers not from the inside but the outside.

One of the federal government's arguments for its liberal immigration policy is that letting more people into this country doesn't add numbers, but just transfers them from, say Mexico, to the United States. What that reasoning overlooks is that once here, the immigrant population begins doing what other Americans do: consuming an undue share of natural resources.

According to the World Resources Institute in Washington, D.C., U.S. citizens consume 43 times as much petroleum per person as people living in India do. That means people in this country, including immigrants, are responsible for creating 19 times more carbon dioxide than the average person in India. Another study showed that the average American has 30 times more impact on the environment than does a person living in a developing country.

A major reason millions of people want to immigrate to the United States is so they, too, can indulge in our over-consumptive lifestyle. Once they arrive, that's just what they do. Roy Beck writes, "Adding one immigrant to the U.S. is the global environmental equivalent of adding two or three dozen people to poor countries."

Studies indicate that immigrants coming here from less developed nations move from being grain eaters to meat consumers. Where they walked or rode buses in their native lands, they drive cars here. While in their own country, they used one gallon of water a day; once they move to the United States, the average goes up to 50 gallons of water every day. Roy Beck summarizes it this way:

> The U.S., because of its size and consumption habits, is the most destabilizing entity within Earth's fragile ecosystem. Population growth here has a far more profound impact on that ecosystem than growth elsewhere.

An argument pro-immigration forces assert is that all national borders are arbitrary, having been set over the centuries through war and acquisitions. Beck's response is:

> The whole human social structure would collapse if everybody asserted a right to reclaim ancestral lands either by changing the borders or by open immigration.

Beck goes on to write what all civilized nations have long accepted:

> Control over entry by non-citizens is generally considered one of the two or three universal attributes of national sovereignty...

Even the poorest third-world country considers its own borders sacred. The 150 poorest nations believe it is their sovereign right to let people in or keep them out of their country.

The other most repeated argument for liberal immigration into this country is that it is the humanitarian thing to do. Because we are a rich country, we need to let the poor come live here too. We also, this argument runs, need to raise the standard of living in those poor countries so they won't want to leave their homelands. But Beck points out that we have proof this does not work.

For forty years, we have sent enormous amounts of aid to third-world nations, but the pressure to immigrate here has only increased. The immigration advocates go on to argue that if we only devoted *enough* money to these 150 poor countries, their birth rates will automatically fall and their living standards rise. So far, that hasn't happened.

The downside of that dubious theory is that by banking on a distant future where Sudanese might want to stay in Sudan, the current liberal immigration policy continues to deteriorate our environment; too many people are coming here to draw on our finite natural resources.

The business interests in this country must think of America's interests first and foremost. Companies have to make a profit to exist, but they also have the responsibility of increasing the health and welfare of the community where the hardworking citizens who live there are making those profits happen. We need to care for our own citizens before we try to save the rest of the world.

There must be a balance among business interests, educational systems, and human health. We must have a system that creates a healthy and prosperous community based on the livability of a safe environment. I call it Economicology. This means meeting human needs has to go hand in hand with meeting business needs. The welfare of every family living in the community depends on this principle of economicology.

In 1973, I wrote to then Michigan Governor William G. Milliken about my fears and my hopes for the future of the planet. That letter was still relevant enough 35 years later to be read in spring of 2008 to a group of Honors Students starting an Economicology School in the Grand Rapids Public Schools system. I knew in 1973, and it's far truer now, that technology could be both a blessing and a curse to us. In man's selfish arrogance, he too often sees it only for how it can improve our lifestyle without thinking about the long-term consequences.

My 1973 letter:

> We are now at a period in which we must assess the effects of the (technological) machinations and stop behaving as though we are the last few generations to inhabit the Earth.

While life was simpler in 1973 – homes and cars were smaller, we drank from the tap instead of polluting with plastic bottles, and people did not have so much "stuff." Even then I worried about the extravagant consuming habits Roy Beck writes about.

Again from my letter:

We must try to change a lifestyle which accepts ugliness as a way of life in our cities, pollution of our atmosphere, and water as if there was an unlimited supply. Social attitudes seem to be more concerned with things than with human beings.

What I advocated 35 years ago I still fight for. We must practice economicology by striking a balance between the needs of our ecology and our economy. Over those 35 years, I have consistently said and written that overpopulation is the greatest threat to the survival of the Earth and all life on it. I have summarized some of Roy Beck's thinking to emphasize this point through his perspective of this country's over-liberal immigration policy.

It seems fitting to end this chapter with the same words I wrote in 1973 to end that letter – words that offer us hope.

> In order to (accomplish these environmental and human goals), we must have a plan. Not a plan to be formulated and put on the shelf, but a plan that must be acceptable to the community and implemented by the political and social forces to make it a reality
>
> In this plan, we must have the courage to believe that economic and technologic considerations must be given equal billing with human needs. In this search for a new social ethic, we will have to base it on a balance of nature with an understanding of the finite world as it really is, not what man conceives it to be.

Peter M. Wege

Reeds Lake, photo taken by Peter M. Wege

CHAPTER 22

Overpopulation: The Greatest Threat to Survival

I wrote about Thomas L. Friedman's book *The World is Flat* back in Chapter 12. In that 2005 book, Friedman said that the world has grown "flat" because advancing communications technology has linked all nations on the planet to the same sources of instant information. One result is that people in undeveloped countries now see all the excess goods citizens in the developed world own and they want the same amount of "stuff." One major problem with this global spreading of materialism is that the Earth's natural resources cannot support such a wealth of consumer goods for every one of the 6.8 billion people on the planet.

In Chapter 10, E.O. Wilson pointed out that every citizen in the United States requires 24 acres of land to supply the food, water, waste, recreation, and government to maintain that one person's lifestyle, while around the world, filling those same needs requires only 2.5 acres – two hugely disproportionate statistics. In order to supply the wish lists of material goods coming from the world's poorer nations, we'd have to come up with four more Earths. In other words, it can't be done.

In 2008, Thomas Friedman published a sort of sequel to *The World Is Flat* adding two adjectives to the title: *Hot, Flat, and Crowded.* In this book, Friedman reiterates his thesis that information technology has flattened the world by expanding the middle class.

A larger middle class around the globe means an increase of material consumption everywhere, not just in the West and in developed countries.

He adds the adjective "hot" to the description of the planet, referring to the environmental damage of global warming. Finally, his third title description of our Earth is "crowded," referring to the explosive population growth we are facing.

Since I have argued for 40 years that overpopulation is the Earth's most dangerous challenge, I am most interested in that "crowded" part of Friedman's new book. The extensive research Thomas Friedman has done on predicting population growth confirms what I've written about since 1968. We are reproducing too fast for the good of this one planet we all need for life. Thomas Friedman writes:

> By 2053, the United Nations projects that there will be more than nine billion people on the planet, thanks to improvements in health care, disease eradication, and economic development. That means in my lifetime the world's population will have more than tripled, and roughly as many people will be born between now and 2053 as were here when I was born (1953.)

The statistics he quotes are frightening. With 6.8 billion people already alive today, Friedman notes that by 2050, according to United Nations projections, that number will grow to 9.2 billion. Friedman writes:

> This increase is equivalent to the total size of the world population in 1950, and it will be absorbed mostly by the less developed regions, whose population is projected to rise from 5.4 billion in 2007 to 7.9 billion in 2050.... So if you think the world feels crowded now, just wait a few decades.

Friedman goes on to note that in 1800, London was the largest city in the world with one million people.

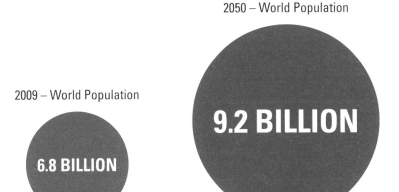

2050 – World Population

9.2 BILLION

2009 – World Population

6.8 BILLION

By 1960, we had 111 cities with over one million residents. Just 35 years later, by 1995, there were 280 cities that big. Today we have over 300 cities with over one million inhabitants, according to U.N. Population Fund statistics.

As I have noted several times, we now have 6.8 billion people drawing on the natural resources of one planet. The best estimates indicate a global population of over nine billion by 2050 – that is a 40 to 45 percent increase! This means even more massive crowding in the poorest cities of the world. That reality is as much a matter of our national security as it is of the environment.

No less than the top man in the Central Intelligence Agency is as worried about global overpopulation as I am! According to General Michael Hayden, director of the CIA, this uncontrolled population growth will happen in the world's poorest countries that are least equipped to support it. Dirty, crowded cities teeming with thirsty, hungry, and poor families are already a breeding ground for terrorists and radical movements.

The intelligence chief named the nations where he sees the greatest threats to world peace already unfolding: Afghanistan, Liberia, Niger, the Democratic

Republic of the Congo, as well as Ethiopia, Nigeria, and Yemen.

Friedman quotes CIA chief General Hayden:

> All those countries will therefore have...a large concentration of young people. If their basic freedoms and basic needs – food, housing, education, employment – are not met, they could be easily attracted to violence, civil unrest, and extremism.

The Hamas rocket attacks on Israel in late 2008 that triggered full-scale warfare against the Palestinians in Gaza is exactly what General Hayden wrote about.

For many years, I have named overpopulation as the single worst threat to humanity and to the planet. But the leaders of those countries with the highest birth rates are not getting the message. If this problem is not addressed soon, civilization faces the worst catastrophe in world history.

This threat to our county's national security, world peace, and the survival of the planet is likely to occur in the largest of urban centers known as "megacities." The statistics on the uptick in the number of mega-cities is another disastrous consequence of overpopulation. Megacities – urban centers with ten million or more people – numbered only five in the whole world in 1975. By 1995, 20 short years later, there were 14 megacities.

Today the U.N. predicts that by 2015 – only five years away – we will have 26 such over-crowded cities around the world. This will have a disastrous effect on growing enough food to feed the whole world. That is a devastating thought and a reliable prediction.

But as I have written and said all along, we must remain positive despite the seriousness of the threat to our planet caused, by too many people. Since starting The Wege Foundation in 1968, I have believed we can make a difference. I would not have supported every cause I have over the last 41 years if I didn't have faith that good people in our country can lead the way out of the massive threats we face. If I didn't have hope that, working together, we can prevent the destruction of our Earth and civilization I would not be writing this second ECONOMICOLOGY book.

That is another reason I urge you to read *Hot, Flat, and Crowded.* Tom Friedman is an optimist just like me. Friedman writes:

> America has a problem and the world has a problem. America's problem is that it has lost its way in recent years – partly because of 9/11 and partly because of the bad habits that we have let build up over the last three decades...

The unscrupulous lending policies of some of our nation's major bank corporations that caused our current financial crisis is an example of our "bad habits." Their greed, along with that of other CEOs in the financial world, has cost unsuspecting Americans their homes to foreclosure.

I agree with Friedman that America needs to find its way again. I keep saying that we have only one chance to change the world. That one chance is based on Economicology: the right balance between economics and ecology.

Friedman shares my belief that our nation can do what has to be done to save the planet. But that means keeping the pressure on our elected officials in Washington to pass legislation that protects this country and its natural resources. As Friedman says:

> When the public is engaged, as it was after 1973 (the first gas shortage), when people were waiting in lines for gasoline, it can override the entrenched interest of the auto and oil lobbies. But the minute...the public takes its eye off the ball, those special interest lobbyists barge back into

the cloakrooms of Congress, passing out political donations and calling the shots according to THEIR needs, not the nation's. What was good for General Motors was not always good for America...

When my father, Peter Martin Wege, came to Grand Rapids to found The Metal Office Furniture Company in 1912, the planet supported the world's population of just over 1.65 million people. The planet has not gotten any bigger, but today 6.8 billion draw on its natural resources for survival! If we are to save our civilization, the United Nations must do a better job in promoting family planning.

In 1972, my friend and environmental hero John W. Gardner published a small book title *In Common Cause: Citizen Action and How It Works.* What he wrote 35 years ago is just as relevant as if he'd published it today. I can't think of a better way to close this chapter than by quoting John W. Gardner's visionary wisdom.

> The citizen can bring our political and governmental institutions back to life, make them responsive and accountable, and keep them honest. No one else can. The one condition for the rebirth of this nation is a rebirth of individual responsibility.

> John W. Gardner

Peter M. Wege's father and mother Peter Martin & Sophia Louise Wege
in 1942 on Lake Leelanau, Michigan, photo courtesy of The Wege Foundation

Epilogue

We have only one world. We have only one life.
Let's keep them both clean. Environmental economy is needed to sustain the growth of everything
on land and sea.

Peter M. Wege

Of the many economicology topics I have touched
on in this book, two themes seem to prevail: the
need to protect the Great Lakes' freshwater and the
global need to control the growth of population. From
H.G. Wells to Rachel Carson to Peter Annin, these
writers consistently present the dangers we face
from our diminishing supply of fresh water. From
Gus Speth to Lindsey Grant to Tom Friedman, these
writers warn about too many people drawing on finite
natural resources.

One solution to save our water is to raise the cost of
water high enough so that we Americans learn how to
conserve this life-sustaining liquid rather than waste it
as we do now. If we are to become good stewards of
the planet's finite freshwater resource, we must begin
now. In pricing the water we now take for granted in
our own homes, municipalities must include the cost
of purifying the water for human consumption. By
increasing our water bills every month, we will also
encourage people to buy water conserving toilets.
Eventually, all toilets will have to be waterless.

Controlling population growth requires educating

people on family planning. These two major themes I keep returning to are interrelated. When we consider the growing population around the world, we realize the possibility of fighting wars over fresh water is very real. The connection between water and population growth is too often overlooked.

Perhaps the worst mistake we've made is damming up our rivers.

For instance, residents in the western United States don't seem to realize they will not have enough fresh water to sustain that fast growing part of the country. Too often, local governments don't recognize the seriousness of the increasing numbers of citizens drawing on a fixed amount of fresh water. This is despite the medical community pronouncement that without fresh water for drinking, we would have less than a week of healthy life.

One reason our country so naturally rich in fresh water now faces a crisis is that we have mismanaged our valuable sources of water. Perhaps the worst mistake we've made is damming up our rivers.

Almost none of the water from the Colorado and Rio Grande rivers ever reaches the Pacific Ocean where they once flowed. The federal government is not doing its part because of the tremendous cost for removing the dams. As Dr. David Ehrenfeld noted in his book *The Arrogance of Humanism,* the completion of the Aswan High Dam in Egypt stopped the Nile from flowing freely; today much less of it empties into the Mediterranean Sea.

Peter Gleick, quoted in this book, is also a co-founder of the Pacific Institute for Studies of Development, Environment, and Security. Gleick has come up with a formula for determining how much fresh water a person needs each day to survive. Gleick cites four water basic needs: drinking, sanitation, bathing, and cooking.

As I reflect on both this book and my first book on economicology, I come back to one of my favorite environmental thinkers, Herman Daly. In 1977, ten years after I started The Wege Foundation, Daly wrote a book called *Steady State Economics.* Like John Gardner, Daly was way ahead of his time. In the economic recession of 2009, Daly's warning that our passion for unrestricted growth and consumption would ultimately destroy the human race seems far too real. Daly defined GNP not as Gross National Product, but as Gross National Cost!

Daly argued that the popular economic indicator should be named for what it really measures – not the merchandise we manufacture, but the cost to make it. The more products we create, the more we drain our finite resources. Indeed, the law of conservation of matter and energy should remind us that real output cannot continuously increase without a matching increase in real input. If we go on building more and bigger products, we will go on using up more and bigger chunks of our natural resources.

Steady-state economics, according to Daly, meaning a constant supply of physical wealth, or capital, needs to be matched by a constant stock of people. But an overstock of people and excessive consumption, Daly warned, will drain away our natural capital – our natural resources. Over 30 years later, we are sadly proving how prophetic Daly was.

Our world faces the disaster of overpopulation along with our own nation's over-consumption – remember the four extra Earths we'd need if everybody on the planet consumed as much as we Americans do? We seem to think unrestrained growth is part of the American dream even as it destroys our natural resources!

We must first reduce our use of non-renewable resources by drastically cutting back our status-seeking, conspicuous consumption. In doing so, we will rediscover the simpler pleasures of the natural world that are now blotted out by our excessive materialism.

Remember that within the lifetime of everyone over 40 years old, world population has doubled. The one natural resource most at risk from this excessive population is fresh water. Our fellow citizens living in the western United States don't seem to realize they will not have enough fresh water to sustain that fast growing part of the country. Unfortunately, neither do their local governments recognize the seriousness of the increasing numbers of citizens drawing on a fixed amount of fresh water. Without fresh water for drinking, human beings have less than a week of healthy life. Peter Gleick, quoted in this book, writes that the four basic water needs for a healthy life include drinking, sanitation, bathing, and cooking.

Now I am not naïve enough to think all you readers of this book will be inspired to change your living habits because of what I've said here. But I do hope the intelligence of the authors I have written about in this *ECONOMICOLOGY II* will spur your interest.

And the blueprint for citizen involvement was written in 1972 by my friend and environmental hero John W. Gardner. Gardner published a small book titled, *In Common Cause: Citizen Action and How It Works*. What he wrote 35 years ago is just as relevant as if he'd published it today. Gardner wrote:

> The citizen can bring our political and governmental institutions back to life, make them responsive and accountable, and keep them honest. No one else can. The one condition for the rebirth of this nation is a rebirth of individual responsibility.

Our citizens need to follow Gardner's wisdom while there's still time to practice economicology. The great thinker and historian H.G. Wells called for such human activism and collaboration on a global scale almost a century ago. In his book *Caring For Creation,* H.G.

Wells proved his brilliance and prophetic wisdom. If all the foundations and charities could come together like H.G. Wells' "world brain" suggested, I know a new form of economic humanness could emerge. Global morality and ethics would begin to push economicology into mainstream thinking. A set of world ethics would spur people to unite against the environmental threats to the entire Earth.

Renewing our relationship with the natural world would contribute to this movement against environmental destruction. In the book *The Ten Trusts* by Jane Goodall and Marc Bekoff we are reminded about the joy in loving nature's animals. Jane Goodall, best known for her work with chimpanzees in Tanzania's Gombe National Park, and Marc Bekoff, an authority on animal behavior, tell us how we can learn from the animals who are part of the one natural whole that includes humans. Goodall and Bekoff write:

> Children brought up in a caring family that respects animals...tend to be kind to animals as adults and to be loving and compassionate individuals.... Children's relationships to animals, then, can be a measure of teaching compassion and kindness...

Certainly no cell phone or iPod ever taught young people how to be kind!

In 1975, Wilson Clark wrote *Energy for Survival: The Alternative to Extinction* where he directed his thoughts to our children and grandchildren:

> In the mad rush to plunder the earth of its dwindling store of non-renewable resources, the leaders of today have forgotten to make room for future generations. The time for change is not some nebulous future date, but now.

We can no longer confine our thinking to the community in which we live; we must extend our perspective to the "big picture" of our planet's capacity to support growing populations in a sustainable manner. Sustainability must be the driving force of this century. We must learn to live with the natural system of the earth. Not until the rest of us also truly understand the natural system can we hope to survive. So how do we go about this tremendous task?

With our world in turmoil over natural resources and political upheaval, the natural way of green living must be studied around the globe. If civilization is not only to survive in its present form, but also to evolve into an even higher form, we must educate, educate, educate. If civilization is to survive, war must end, and the intelligent leaders of this world must come together for the best interests of the entire planet, home Earth!

It is time for the world's major religions to join together if we are to solve the greatest environmental threat to our Earth: overpopulation. Every country that is out of balance with its natural resources has to reduce its birth rates. We must begin to limit the population worldwide, and educating the leaders on that essential truth must start now.

The 1991 book *Saving the Planet* put out by the Worldwatch Environmental Series says this on how to help solve the education problem:

> According to the World Bank, providing elementary education for the estimated 120 million school-age children not now in school around the world would cost roughly fifty dollars each, or six billion dollars per year. Providing literacy training for illiterate women who are beyond school age would require an additional estimated two billion dollars annually.

All people in the world want a quality environment to live in. All of us want our children to grow up healthy, with love and compassion. Overpopulation can destroy that dream for everyone unless we do something about it now. Education is the key to family planning which will prevent us from populating ourselves into extinction.

But this environmentally-driven, conserving, and simplifying technology won't happen on its own. What will force us to make these changes will be disasters caused by the very over-consumption we economicologists know must be curbed. Our extravagant waste of fossil fuels created the shortages that sent gas prices over four dollars a gallon. Only when it hurt their wallets at the gas pump did owners of fuel-guzzling SUVs start looking at hybrids and other smaller, more fuel efficient cars.

This process of caring about the human race has been a running battle for the last millennium. We should have started putting the principles of economicology in practice right after the disaster of World War II. Today we are at a point where within the next few years we face a loss of energy to sustain our living habits.

Our fellow citizens living in the western United States don't seem to realize they will not have enough fresh water to sustain that fast growing part of the country.

A major first step to survival could be simply, "Educate, Don't Propagate." There is only so much water and so much land on this planet, and unless we control the population level, we will not have enough of those two resources necessary to sustain human life. Without a thorough understanding of Earth's life-support system, we won't solve the problem of overpopulation in the foreseeable future.

What is needed above all is compassion and understanding. Some things are best said in poetry.

Dedicated to an Angel Called Hope,
Prayer for Compassion and Understanding

Oh Lord, God –

We pray that you will address our human
weaknesses and give us the strength to
understand our frailties.

What are we doing to the life-support system
you gave us, the clean air, clean water of a
healthy existence?

We have fouled our life-support system by
human ignorance and the pursuit of personal
achievements and unreliable goals, which cause
human greed instead of need.

Give us compassion and understanding of why
we are here on this dot in the Universe.

We have lost touch with you, Lord, and beg
that you bring us back to the realization

That we need to grow a healthy mind, body,
and spirit

In your name. Amen.

By Peter M. Wege

My prayer is that the collective wisdom contained
in this second ECONOMICOLOGY book will fire
up readers to fight the good environmental fight
while there's still time. This book is the story of the
Six Es that will determine our future. It is about the
inseparability of Economics, Environment, Ecology,
Ethics, Empathy, and Education. All the brilliant writers
you met on these pages fit into the mosaic of this "E
to the Sixth Power."

My mission in this second book has been to
convince you, the reader, that what is said here really

matters. I have quoted great environmental thinkers to help present my case for the good of the planet. Getting your attention has been my first challenge. The second is getting you to respond to realities that could save the system which nurtures and sustains us all.

I first heard this concept of a holistic approach to environmentalism at my son's graduation from Williams College in 1972. The renowned microbiologist René Dubos gave the commencement address that afternoon. Now, almost 40 years later, I still feel privileged to have heard his message. Speaking as a scientist, René Dubos described the oneness of all living things. Dubos told the college graduates that this unity of all life required each of us as human beings to accept responsibility for taking care of the living earth.

As Dubos put it:

> Man possesses the power to change the living earth which nurtures and shapes man and determines his fate. They are thereby complementary components of a system. Each shapes the other in a continuous act of creation.

Indeed, René Dubos' intelligent grasp of environmental issues so impressed me that I borrowed from the following sentence to subtitle my first book on ECONOMICOLOGY. Dubos wrote, "To strive for environmental quality could be considered the eleventh commandment."

The book I published, *ECONOMICOLOGY: The Eleventh Commandment,* in 1998, followed up on René Dubos' quotation. My version of the Eleventh Commandment is this: *Thou shalt not commit abuse against the environment, but rather honor it with respect for sustaining life as we know it.* My theory for how we must proceed to sustain life is summarized in the title of that first book and the one you are reading: "economicology."

Speaking at Williams College that day, René Dubos recognized that without a healthy ecology, we can't have a healthy economy. The great microbiologist thus spoke to the truth of economicology's philosophy. Taking care of the ecology is also taking care of the economy.

> If civilization is to survive, war must end, and
> the intelligent leaders of this world must come
> together for the best interests of the entire
> planet, our home Earth!

Peter M. Wege

Peter M. Wege, photo courtesy of The Wege Foundation

Bibliography

& Recommended Reading

Alexander, Jeff
Michigan State University Press

Pandora's Locks
2009

Allen, William
Oxford University Press

*Green Phoenix: Restoring the
Tropical Forests of Guanacaste,
Costa Rica*
2003

Anderson, Ray C.
Chelsea Green

Mid-Course Correction
1998

Annin, Peter
Island Press

The Great Lakes Water Wars
2006

Ashworth, William
Wayne State University Press

The Late, Great Lakes
1987

Ayres, Ed
Four Walls Eight Windows

God's Last Offer
1999

Beck, Roy
Contract Press

Re-Charting America's Social
Future
1994

Bekoff, Marc & Jane Goodall
HarperCollins

*The Ten Trusts : What We
Must Do to Care for the
Animals We Love*
2003

Brown, Lester R.
W.W. Norton & Company

*PLAN B: Rescuing a Planet
under Stress and a Civilization
in Trouble*
2003

Brown, Lester R.
W.W. Norton & Company

PLAN B 2.0: Rescuing a
Planet Under Stress and a
Civilization in Trouble
2006

Brown, Lester & Christopher Flavin
W.W. Norton & Company

Saving the Planet: How to
Shape an Environmentally
Sustainable Global Economy
1991

Brown, Peter & Geoffrey Garver
Berrett-Koehler Publishers

Right Relationship: Building a
Whole Earth Economy
2009

Carson, Rachel
Mariner Books

Silent Spring
2002

Collier, Michael & Robert H. Webb
University of Arizona Press

Floods, Droughts, and
Climate Change
2002

Daly, Herman E.
Beacon Press

Beyond Growth
1996

Daly, Herman E.
W.H. Freeman

Steady State Economics
1977

Dempsey, Dave
Michigan State University Press

On the Brink
2004

Dubos, René
Columbia University Press

Reason Awake
1970

Ehrenfeld, David
Oxford University Press

Arrogance of Humanism
1989

Friedman, Thomas L.
Farrar, Straus & Giroux

Hot, Flat, and Crowded
2008

Friedman, Thomas L.
Farrar, Straus & Giroux

The World is Flat
2008

Gardner, John W.
W.W. Norton & Company

*In Common Cause: Citizen
Action and How It Works*
1971

Gardner, John W.
Jossey-Bass

*Living, Leading and the
American Dream*
2003

Gardner, John W.
Free Press / Macmillan Company

On Leadership
1990

Gardner, John W.
W.W. Norton & Company

Self-Renewal
1981

Gardner, John W. / Task Force
on Environmental Health &
Related Problems
Government Printing Office:
Washington D.C.

*A Strategy for a Livable
Environment*

1967

Goodell, Jeff
Houghton Mifflin Company

*Big Coal: The Dirty Secret
Behind America's Energy
Future*
2007

Gorz, Andre
South End Press

Ecology as Politics
1980

Grant, Lindsey
Seven Locks Press

Too Many People
2000

Hartmann, Thom
Three Rivers Press

*The Last Hours of Ancient
Sunlight*
1999

Hartung, William D.
HarperCollins

And Weapons for All
1994

Hawken, Paul
HarperBusiness

The Ecology of Commerce
1993

Hawken, Paul, Amory &
L. Hunter Lovins
Little, Brown & Company

Natural Capitalism

1999

Henderson, Hazel
Kumarian Press

Beyond Globalization
1999

Johnson, Huey P.
University of Nebraska

Green Plans
1997

Kennedy, Robert F., Jr.
HarperCollins

Crimes Against Nature
2002

Magee, Mike
Spencer Books

The Book of Choices
2002

Muldoon, Paul & Lee Botts
Michigan State University Press

*Evolution of The Great Lake
Water Quality Agreement*
2005

Orr, David W.
Island Press

Earth in Mind
2004

Princen, Thomas, Michael
Maniales & Ken Conca
The MIT Press

Confronting Consumption

2002

Reece, Erik
Riverhead Books

*Lost Mountain: A Year in
the Vanishing Wilderness*
2006

Shnayerson, Michael
Vanity Fair

"The Rape Of Appalachia"
May, 2006

Speth, James Gustave
Yale University Press

Red Sky at Morning
2004

Wells, H.G.
Longmans, Green & Company

Fate of Man
1939

Wilson, E.O.
Vintage Books / Random House

Consilience
1998

Wilson, E.O.
W.W. Norton & Company

*The Creation: An Appeal
to Save Life on Earth*
2006

Wilson, E.O.
Alfred A. Knopf

The Future of Life
2002